Shabbat Shalom

Insights on the Weekly Torah Portion from the Heart of Biblical Israel

By

Sondra Oster Baras

Israeli Director of Christian Friends of Israeli Communities

For More Information
Please visit
WWW.CFOIC.COM

Shabbat Shalom

Insights on the Weekly Torah Portion from the Heart of Biblical Israel

By

Sondra Oster Baras

Christian Friends of Israeli Communities

Edited by

Rabbi Tuly Weisz

Israel 365

Table of Contents

EXODUS – SHEMOT

LEVITICUS – VAYIKRA

NUMBERS – BAMIDBAR

DEUTERONOMY – DEVARIM

Sondra Oster Baras, Samaria

Introduction

I had already been speaking to Christian audiences about Israel for many years when one of my Christian colleagues suggested that I share Bible teachings on a regular basis with our Christian audience. Although my frequent lectures to Christians, both in Israel and around the world, often included Biblical teachings, as I connected the realities of modern life in Israel with the ancient Biblical principles, I was rather surprised at the notion that Christians might be interested in regular teachings on the Portion of the Week from an Orthodox Jew.

Years later, I can safely say that my weekly Bible teachings, both in print and in video, have met a demand that we are only beginning to appreciate. Pastors have told me that they incorporate some of my teachings in their sermons. I have had many exciting conversations with Christian friends and colleagues on points of Biblical interpretation. What has characterized all of these encounters, however, has been an honest quest for understanding and knowledge among my Christian friends.

For centuries, Jews have not only read the Torah portion each week but the words of the weekly portion have focused family discussions and weekly Bible classes alike in Jewish communities all over the world. We have a long tradition of Biblical exegesis, dating back to the Second Temple Period, and we continue to study the ancient commentaries, combined with more modern interpretations on a regular basis. As a Jew, I have taken this type of study for granted. Through my encounters with Christians who share the same Biblical text but who have not been privy to the same interpretative tradition, I have come to realize how rich our tradition really is. And I have been privileged to be invited to share this tradition with so many non-Jews around the world.

This book is a collection of many of these weekly teachings. They reflect my own thoughts and interpretations but draw heavily on the traditions of the classic commentaries and Midrash, the oldest of the exegetical texts. Jewish commentary invites dialogue with the text, encourages questions and answers, and reflects a drive to attain greater understanding while accepting the divinity and authority of the text. I have tried to communicate my love for the Bible through these following essays and hope they will serve to stimulate broader discussion and interpretation of the Bible, within the context of our collective human endeavor to better understand God.

I would like to thank my colleagues Kimberly Troup and Shira Schwartz who helped me with this project, who read the texts, offered comments, and especially assisted in finding appropriate photographs. And I want to especially thank all those who sent me photographs over the years, of the people and communities in Judea and Samaria and of those who love Israel everywhere. Your photographs are what make this book so special!

Sondra Oster Baras
Christian Friends of Israeli Communities,
Karnei Shomron, Samaria, Israel

He told his nation the power of his actions
to bequeath them the inheritance of nations. (PSALMS 111:6)

Sunrise over the Samarian Mountains

Bereisheet

Genesis 1:1 – 6:8

The designation of the Land of Israel to the Jewish people is fundamental to the Bible. It is the foundation upon which the entire text stands!

"*In the beginning God created the heavens and the earth*" (Genesis 1:1). The Bible opens with the book of Genesis, and its first words determine its essence – the beginning. The beginning of time, the beginning of the world, the beginning of mankind. It is these first chapters of the Bible that lay the foundation for all that comes later. Essentially, however, the Book of Genesis tells the story of the family of Abraham ending with the sons of Jacob who go down to Egypt and whose descendants leave that country as a nation, the Children of Israel. The foundational chapters of Genesis, therefore, tell us something of the history of Abraham's family, tracing his roots back to Adam and providing us with the list of each generation between Adam and Abraham. And the Book of Genesis, itself, forms the foundation of the People of Israel for whom the Bible has been written, to whom it has been given and whose story it tells.

But is this lengthy introduction necessary? If, indeed, the purpose of the Bible is to tell the story of Israel, why must it begin with creation? Rashi, an 11th century rabbi and brilliant scholar and one of the most widely studied of the traditional commentaries, asks a similar question. He notes that, arguably, the Bible should not have begun with Genesis at all, but with the first commandment given to the Jewish people – the declaration of the new month (EXODUS 12:2). If, indeed, the purpose of the Bible is to teach us how to behave and how to obey God, it should restrict itself to a list of commandments and to those stories that illustrate how those commandments are kept and the covenantal relationship between God and His people.

Rashi provides a stunning answer – ***"Because of the Scripture*** (PSALMS 111:6) ***'He told his nation the power of his actions to bequeath them the inheritance of nations.' So that if the nations were to accuse Israel of stealing the land from the seven nations, Israel should respond as follows: 'The earth belongs to God, He created it and gave it to whomever he wished. When it was His will, He gave it to them (the seven nations) and when He wished, He took it from them and gave it to us.'"***

The only reason that God bothered to write the details of creation and the stories of the early patriarchs and biblical heroes was to solidify His claim to the Land of Israel, and, in turn, the claim of His people to the land. In other words, the Bible doesn't merely record the fact of God's giving of the land to the People of Israel. Rather, the designation of the Land of Israel to the Jewish people is fundamental to the Bible. It is the foundation upon which the entire text stands!

The verse in Psalms noted by Rashi is a powerful Scriptural anchor for this concept. But there is an even better one. In the Song of Moses at the end of Deuteronomy, Moses proclaims:

"When the Most High gave to the nations their inheritance, when he divided mankind, He fixed the borders of the peoples according to the number of the Children of Israel" (DEUTERONOMY 32:8).

This Scripture is referring to God's initial division of mankind into nations which takes place at the Tower of Babel:

"These are the clans of the sons of Noah, according to their genealogies, in their nations, and from these the nations spread abroad on the earth after the flood... So the Lord dispersed them from there over the face of all the earth, and they left off building the city. Therefore its name was called Babel, because there the Lord confused the language of all the earth. And from there the Lord dispersed them over the face of all the earth." (Genesis 10:32, 11:8-9)

From one people who united for an evil purpose, God created the nations, giving each his own language, national identity and land, as detailed in Genesis 10. This happened just a few generations after the Flood. There was no Abraham and the Bible had not yet mentioned anything about the Land of Israel or the People of Israel. But the above verse in Deuteronomy makes it clear that God had already designated the Land of Israel for the People of Israel when He created the other nations and gave them their lands.

God's designation of the People of Israel, whose rightful place is the Land of Israel and whose purpose is to obey and proclaim the God of Israel, is established at the beginning of time. When God recorded His words in the Bible for eternity, He established Himself as Creator in order to validate this designation.

Before the Bible becomes a Jewish book,
it must lay the foundations for all of humanity.

Special-needs Children at Heart of Benjamin in Ofra

NOACH

GENESIS 6:9 – 11:32

Noah is the transitional character between early man who learns how to survive as a human being, and Abraham, who learns what it is to be chosen by God.

"These are the generations of Noah. Noah was a righteous man, perfect in his generation." (GENESIS 6:9) This week's Torah portion begins with the introduction of Noah. Interestingly, the portion does not begin with the first verse of chapter 6 which sets forth the story of the sons of the judges taking the daughters of man and the ensuing corruption of society. Even though verse 8 mentions Noah, it is verse 9 that introduces Noah as a main character and begins this week's portion: ***"These are the generations of Noah"*** (GENESIS 6:9). Noah, and his progeny, are the main focus of this week's portion.

The portion contains two main stories, that of the Flood and that of the Tower of Babel, as well as a list of generations which link Noah with Abraham. Indeed, if I were to characterize this Torah portion, it would be the story of the transition between the first generations of man, Adam and Eve and their descendants, and Abraham, the man who begins the story of the Jewish people. The first Torah portion of the cycle, Bereisheet, discusses a pre-historic period, depicting Adam and Eve, their children and the first generations following, which are mentioned briefly and with little detail. Most reflect archetypal characters – the first murderer, the first metal worker, the first musician and the first man ***"who walked with God"*** (Enoch). Beginning with next week's portion, we learn the history of the Jewish people beginning with Abraham, the first man whom God chooses and who will be the father of the Jewish people.

In between is Noah. Who then is Noah and what does he represent? Every human being alive today is a son of Noah, as he and his sons were the only human beings to survive the flood, and a new humanity began with him. In Jewish tradition, universal morality or the laws that should govern all civilizations are referred to as Noachide laws, or the rules that apply to the sons of Noah. They include the prohibition against murder and theft, the belief in one God and the obligation to establish a judicial system.

Aside from the technicality of Noah being the father of all humanity, I believe that the character of Noah and the period of time reflected in this week's portion tell us a great deal of what that universal moral code is all about. When God decides to destroy the universe with a great flood, He laments the theft that is rampant in society. People do not respect the property of others, indicating a total breakdown in mankind's respect for his fellow human beings. Society cannot function if man does not respect the dignity and rights of his fellow human being. This, then, is the basis for moral behavior.

After the flood, the new society aims to build a tower of Babel – to reach into the heavens and combat God. Another basis for any society must be humility before God and the recognition that man is subject to God's commandments. Ironically, it was the unity of mankind in furtherance of the objective to rebel against God that provoked God especially – He mixed up their languages so that they could no longer achieve such unity in pursuit of a negative objective.

Beginning with Genesis 12, God speaks specifically to the Jewish people and offers the history of His designation of the Jewish people as His people and the significance of that choice for His people and for humanity. But before the Bible becomes a Jewish book, it must lay the foundations for all of humanity.

Noah is the transitional character between early man who learns how to survive as a human being, and Abraham, who learns what it is to be chosen by God. Noah learns about society, and it is through Noah and through this week's Torah portion, that every human being can draw the lessons that inform all of humanity – human dignity and respect for every human being and the belief in one God. And it is only against this backdrop that the story of the Jewish people can gain relevance for all humanity. For it is only if mankind can respect the different destinies of each nation and individual, and honor and obey God, will mankind understand and respect the role of the Jewish people that God has destined for them.

To your offspring I will give this land. (GENESIS 12:7)

Planting trees in Karnei Shomron

Lech Lecha

Genesis 12:1 – 17:27

Those of us who are convinced that the modern rebirth of Israel is the beginning of the redemption are following the model of Abraham.

This week's Torah portion begins with God's commandment to Abraham to leave his country, his birthplace and his father's home and go forward to ***"the land that I will show you"*** (Genesis 12:1). Verse 3 contains God's promise to bless all those who bless Abraham and to curse all those who curse him: ***"And I will make you a great nation; I will bless those who bless you and curse those who curse you; and all the families of the earth shall bless themselves by you"*** (Genesis 12:3).

Abraham arrives in the Land of Canaan and then, for the first time, God promises ***"To your offspring I will give this land"*** (Genesis 12:7). The drama of this first section of the chapter is incredible. In these few verses, the stage is set for the entire relationship between God, the Nation of Israel and the Land of Israel that is the predominant theme of the rest of the Bible. However, in truth, Abraham's departure for the Land of Canaan does not begin with Genesis 12, but begins in the previous chapter:

"Terah took Abram his son and Lot the son of Haran, his grandson, and Sarai his daughter-in-law, his son Abram's wife, and they went forth together from Ur of the Chaldeans to go into the land of Canaan, but when they came to Haran, they settled there" (Genesis 11:31).

Terah, then, is the initiator of the journey to the Land of Canaan. Of course, he didn't actually arrive in Canaan, because along the way he stopped in Haran and settled there. However, the opening verses of Chapter 12 make it sound as if God is originating something different, a journey never before embarked upon, when in actuality, Terah had already begun the journey on his own, without God's intervention.

The Midrash is replete with stories that explain the sequence of events that involve both Terah and Abraham's journey. There is an ancient tradition of Abraham confronting Nimrod, King of the Chaldeans, where Nimrod represents the pagan beliefs of the time and Abraham, the belief in one God. Nimrod, angered by Abraham's refusal to believe in his gods, throws Abraham into a great furnace, but Abraham miraculously walks out unscathed. Some of the stories, therefore, see Terah as leaving Ur right after this event, with Abraham and the entire family in tow, in order to avoid the continued wrath of Nimrod and the Chaldeans. It is clear, however, that Terah himself is an idol worshipper, both from the Midrash stories and from Joshua 24:2.

It is not clear whether God spoke to Abraham in Ur or in Haran. But I believe that there were two separate motivations for traveling to the Land of Canaan. Terah clearly did not leave Ur in order to obey God – he was interested in protecting his family, seeking greater fortune, or whatever ordinary motivations would lead someone to move to a different land. Abraham, on the other hand, left only because God commanded him to do so. It is possible that Abraham initially left Ur with his father, following along with no other motivation than to join the family. And it is possible that God already spoke to him in Ur. What is clear, however, is that God's message to Abraham was unique, and it is this message we have carried with us ever since.

It is interesting to note that both the Christian monk who divided the Bible into chapters and the Jewish traditions that divided it into weekly portions, started Abraham's story where it is today. Really, it could have begun in verse 27 of the previous chapter, with the language of ***"These are the clans of Terah."*** But instead, both Christian and Jewish traditions believed that Abraham's exit is the true beginning of the story – Terah's exit is something far more ordinary and far less significant.

There is an important lesson for us today in this study. When the Jews first began to return to the Land of Israel in the late 19th and early 20th centuries, most were probably more similar to Terah than to Abraham. They did not hear the call of God, but they did feel the pain of anti-Semitism, not that different from Nimrod's burning hot furnace. The modern State of Israel has always struggled with an ambivalent identity, a safe haven for the Jewish people or the beginning of our national and spiritual redemption as promised by God and foretold by the prophets.

Terah's journey is recorded and it is worthy of note. It is the journey that began Abraham's journey and was relevant to it, otherwise the Bible would not have noted it. Likewise, even the most secular Zionists contributed greatly to Israel. But the focus of Abraham's journey is God's commandment and Abraham's own absolute obedience to that commandment. Today, those of us who are convinced that the modern rebirth of Israel is the ***"beginning of the flowering of the redemption"*** as we recite in our prayers each Shabbat, are following the model of Abraham. And even as we hold on to parts of the land that are controversial, our motivation is the very message that Abraham heard from God, in the center of Samaria: ***"To your offspring I will give this land!"*** It is Abraham's story that begins the chapter and the Torah portion – it is this story that really counts.

I will establish my covenant with him as an everlasting covenant for his offspring after him. (GENESIS 17:19)

Soldier and child at the El Matan pioneering neighborhood of Maale Shomron

Vayerah

Genesis 18:1 – 22:24

God wanted one people to inherit His covenant with Abraham, one people to inherit the Land of Israel, one people to be His people, for eternity.

This week's portion opens with God's appearance to Abraham and the appearance of the three angels. There follows a series of conversations and activities that culminate in the announcement to Abraham that Sarah will bear a son and that his name will be Isaac. It is interesting to note, however, that everything about the announcement of this birth and the birth itself is miraculous and unusual.

Abraham is actually first told of the birth of a son to Sarah in the previous chapter. Just as Abraham is entering into a very special covenant with God, the covenant of circumcision that the Children of Israel will continue for eternity, God promises Abraham that Sarah will have a son, and that God will bless her with nations and kings descending from her (Genesis 17:16). Abraham has trouble believing this promise, as he would be 100 and Sarah 90 when she would give birth. In fact, Abraham argues with God and tells him that Ishmael is his son and he is satisfied with him as an heir. God replies:

"No, but Sarah your wife shall bear you a son, and you shall call his name Isaac. I will establish my covenant with him as an everlasting covenant for his offspring after him." (Genesis 17:19)

And while God promises Abraham that Ishmael will also be a great nation, He makes it very clear that it is Isaac and only Isaac who will inherit God's covenant with Abraham and the special relationship that began in Genesis 12.

In the following chapter, the three angels repeat the promise, but this time Sarah hears it for the first time, overhearing the conversation between Abraham and the angels while she is preparing the meal in the tent. Like Abraham, she has trouble believing it and even laughs. Scripture, once again, makes sure to mention that both Abraham and Sarah are very old and that Sarah no longer has her menses, so that the very idea of her giving birth seems ludicrous. Isaac's name is a derivative of laughter in Hebrew and his name is a reminder of the laughter and disbelief that accompanied both Sarah and Abraham's initial reaction to the idea of his birth.

In fact, as we know, one year later, Isaac is born to Sarah and Abraham and he, indeed, becomes Abraham's one and only heir. We don't know that much about his life, but one incident, of course, stands out – the binding of Isaac. It seems that Isaac's life, including the foretelling of his birth, is a series of unusual occurrences that indicate God's special appointment of him as Abraham's heir. He is born to elderly parents, when it would have been so much simpler for him to have been born years earlier. His birth is announced twice, first by God Himself to Abraham and later by the three angels. And Sarah finds out about the upcoming birth by eavesdropping – not even a direct announcement. The binding of Isaac, of course, is a truly mysterious event, as God commands Abraham to perform the unimaginable only to cancel his order at the last minute. The actual import of that event is beyond the scope of this discussion, but it is one more unusual God-directed event in the life of Isaac.

I believe that Isaac's birth was meant to be unusual, to draw attention, to invite questions and to imply the miraculous. Isaac is the appointed heir of Abraham, the second of three forefathers of the Jewish people. In the natural order of circumstances, Ishmael would have indeed inherited the covenant, for he was the first-born son. But God wanted otherwise. He wanted to appoint the heir and have that heir arrive in this world under miraculous circumstances so that no one would question that this heir was not naturally appointed, but God appointed. And God did not want the inheritance split between two sons – only Isaac would inherit the promise.

God wanted one people to inherit His covenant with Abraham, one people to inherit the Land of Israel, one people to be His people, for eternity. And I thank God, daily, that I have been born to this people. It is a profound responsibility, but it is an honor.

This land was purchased by our forefather as a family burial plot.

The Cave of Machpela, Hebron

Chayei Sara

Genesis 23:1 – 25:18

It is as if God wants to make sure we understand exactly where this purchase is – in Hebron. There is no mistaking it – this land was purchased by our forefather.

This week's Torah reading opens with the death of Sarah, the wife of Abraham, in Hebron (Genesis 23). Abraham mourns his wife and then immediately goes about the business of burying her. He approaches the Hittites, the native residents of Hebron, and identifies himself as a stranger and resident among them, a foreign resident in modern terms. He asks to purchase a piece of land to bury his wife. The Hittites, recognizing Abraham as an important man, offer to allow him to bury his wife on their land, for free. Abraham refuses their offer, however, and insists on purchasing the land at its full price. In fact, he knows exactly which piece of land he wants – the Cave of Machpela and its accompanying field. The purchase is a public affair, carried out at the gates to the city, in the presence of the Hittites.

The transaction is spelled out in great detail, with special emphasis placed on certain words and phrases. In verse 2, we learn that Sarah dies ***"in Kiryat Arba that is, Hebron in the land of Canaan."*** In verse 17, the transaction is sealed and the location of the field and cave are spelled out: ***"The field of Ephron in Machpelah, which was to the east of Mamre, the field with the cave that was in it and all the trees that were in the field, throughout its whole area"*** (Genesis 23:17).

In verse 19, the location is spelled out yet again: ***"the cave of the field of Machpelah east of Mamre that is, Hebron in the land of Canaan."*** It is as if Scripture wants to make sure we realize that Kiryat Arba and Mamre are synonyms for Hebron and that this is in the Land of Canaan. The landmark is so important and its geography is so important – lest we forget!

Unusual emphasis is also placed on the exchange of money: Abraham insists on paying the ***"full price"*** (GENESIS 23:9). In verse 13, Abraham repeats the fact that he is giving money for the purchase. In Verse 16, Abraham transfers ***"four hundred shekels of silver, according to the weights current among the merchants."*** It is almost as if Abraham knows that he had better make sure this transfer is done properly, according to the books, or the land will be taken from him. And the way Scripture records it, is as if God wants to make sure we understand exactly where this purchase is – in Hebron, in the Land of Canaan. There is no mistaking it – this land was purchased by our forefather as a family burial plot.

At the end of the Book of Genesis, the purchase of the Machpela Cave in Hebron is mentioned once more, as Jacob commands his sons to bury him in that very same cave, and yet again, the detail is astounding: ***"Bury me with my fathers in the cave which is in the field of Machpelah, facing Mamre, in the land of Canaan, the field that Abraham bought from Ephron the Hittite for a burial site... the field and the cave in it bought from the Hittites"*** (GENESIS 49:29-32). Jacob, like his father before him, wants to ensure that his sons understand that this land was purchased and belongs to the family.

It is amazing therefore, that one of the most disputed places in Israel today is Hebron. Even as hundreds of Jews live in the old city of Hebron, thousands of Jews live nearby in Kiryat Arba, and tens of thousands live in the surrounding hills of Judea, international opinion dictates that Hebron belongs to the Arabs.

For many years now, a wonderful tradition has developed in Hebron on the Shabbat when we read this Torah portion. Jews from all over Israel converge upon Hebron for this Shabbat. Every home in Kiryat Arba and Jewish Hebron opens its doors to friends and relatives. Teen-agers come from all over the country and sleep on the floors of schools and other public buildings. Shabbat meals are great gatherings and logistical nightmares. No one knows how everyone fits in, but somehow they do. On Shabbat morning, guests and residents alike stream to the Machpela Cave and there, on the very spot where Abraham buried his wife Sarah, the very place which Abraham purchased thousands of years ago, they read this chapter and praise God for His bounty.

The people of Israel must descend from a man who understands the holiness of marriage.

A Jewish wedding in Hebron

Toldot

Genesis 25:19 – 28:9

The people of Israel, the children which Abraham was promised by God, must descend from a man who understands the holiness of relationships.

This week's Torah portion tells the story of the birth of Jacob and Esau and Isaac's blessing of his sons before his death. I would like to focus on this latter story, the story of the switching of the blessings between Jacob and Esau.

Although chapter 27 begins with the description of Isaac's old age and his failed vision, I believe the story actually begins with the previous few verses. Those verses tell of Esau's choosing two Canaanite women as his wives, who cause bitterness to Isaac and Rebekah. The final verse of the portion (Genesis 28:9) describes Esau marrying a daughter of Ishmael, *"Abraham's son."* The implication is obvious. Esau's initial marriage to two Canaanite women upset his parents, as Abraham had ensured that his son not marry a Canaanite woman and Isaac understood and integrated this concept into his own value system. After losing the blessing to Jacob, Esau finally realizes that his parents oppose intermarriage with the Canaanites. In a belated and ineffective attempt to regain his parents' confidence in him, he takes a wife who is a descendant of Abraham.

The issue of Esau's marriages, therefore, forms the framework for the story that develops within – the replacement of Esau by Jacob as the heir and first-born of Isaac. It is interesting to note that Scripture, in describing Esau, never uses the word first-born, but refers to him as the older son (Genesis 27:1, 42). It is only Esau who refers to himself as the first-born (Genesis 27:32). God has made His opinion known – Esau is not Isaac's heir.

Isaac's vision has dimmed, a fact that serves not only to explain how Isaac would have confused his two sons, but that also provides a figurative explanation to a different sort of blindness – Isaac's inability to discern the true character of his son Esau and the fact that it is Jacob who should be his true heir.

Interestingly though, Isaac, confusing Jacob with Esau, blesses Jacob with material wealth and dominance over his brother. But he does not give him the blessing of Abraham, the blessing of children and the Land of Israel. This blessing is held back, bestowed upon Jacob before he leaves for Haran (Genesis 28:4). Probably, Isaac intended to give this blessing to Jacob all along. Perhaps Isaac believed that his two children would share an inheritance, that Esau would have political dominance but that Jacob would be the father of God's people and would possess God's land.

Perhaps it is Esau's choice of wives which enables Isaac to see, from the outset, that Esau will not receive the blessing of Abraham. At the end of the day, the people of Israel, the children which Abraham was promised by God, must descend from a man who understands the holiness of the relationship between man and woman and who marries a woman worthy of that relationship. In the previous Torah portion, we read of Abraham's incredible efforts to select the appropriate wife for Isaac. Esau's marriage to Hitite women enabled both Rebekah and Isaac to understand that Esau could not be Abraham's heir.

Isaac believed, however, that Esau might still attain political dominance. He believed, wrongly, that the chosen people of God would have spiritual dominance without political dominance. Rebekah however, understood that the people of Israel would need both. But as Isaac understood later, in order to sustain both political and spiritual dominance, the Children of Jacob would need to be worthy. Isaac tells Esau: ***"when you grow restless you shall break his yoke from your neck"*** (Genesis 27:40). Rashi, one of the most important of Jewish classical commentators, explains that this refers to Esau seeing Jacob in sin and feeling wronged by the superior blessings that Jacob has received – then, indeed, Jacob will suffer and Esau's power will prevail.

May we indeed be worthy of attaining both spiritual and political dominance as we struggle to hold on to the Land of Israel, first promised to our forefather Abraham as an everlasting inheritance.

Give me children, or I shall die.

Tomb of Rachel, Bethlehem

Vayetzei

Genesis 28:10 – 32:3

Jacob has been promised by God that his children will inherit the Land of Israel. Indeed, he is the first forefather to pass on this promise and blessing to all of his children.

This week's portion tells of Jacob's flight from Beersheba, escaping just in time from his brother Esau who has threatened to kill him. Jacob encounters God in a prophetic dream, just before leaving the Land of Israel, and God promises that He will protect Jacob and return him to his land. He bestows upon Jacob the original promise that He made to Abraham – to give the land to his children: ***"And behold! God was standing over him [Jacob] and He said, I am the Lord, God of Abraham your father and God of Isaac; the ground upon which you are lying, to you will I give it and to your descendants"*** (Genesis 28:13).

Most of the portion, however, deals with Jacob's sojourn with his uncle Laban, a sly and dishonest fellow. Almost overnight, Jacob is transformed from the innocent dweller of tents (Genesis 25:27) to a fugitive from his vengeful brother, to someone who has to learn to outsmart Laban. When he returns to the Land of Israel, he has amassed a fortune in sheep and goats, has escaped unharmed from Laban's reach, and successfully encounters and pacifies Esau. Jacob is, indeed, capable of becoming the father of a great nation.

Central to the portion is the story of Jacob's marriages to Rachel and Leah, and afterwards to their maids Zilpah and Bilhah, and the birth of 12 children, 11 sons and 1 daughter. Leah conceives easily and bears Jacob six children. Rachel is barren until the very end of the story, and then bears Jacob one son – Joseph. (Benjamin is born en route to Israel, as we will read in next week's portion.) Rachel, as the barren mother, follows the pattern that is set earlier with the stories of Sarah and Rebekah, each finding it difficult to conceive a child. Rachel's distress is great and her outburst at her beloved husband Jacob is heartbreaking: ***"Give me children, or I shall die!"*** (GENESIS 30:1). Jacob's response is an angry one: ***"Am I in the place of God, who has withheld from you the fruit of the womb?"*** (GENESIS 30:2).

Rachel wants so badly to have a child. She wants to give birth to Jacob's child; she wants to raise a child; she wants to hold a child in her lap. This passion for a child is so human and so natural, and yet, heart-wrenching all the same. As any woman who has suffered the pain and frustration of infertility will tell you, there is no greater desire of a woman than the desire to bear children. And when pregnancy is not forthcoming, the frustration and physical pain is so deep.

But I believe that the tension that is so palpably felt in the interchange between Jacob and Rachel, takes us beyond the ordinary realm of family relationships. Jacob has been promised by God that he will have children and that they will inherit the Land of Israel. Indeed, he is the first forefather to pass on this promise and blessing to all of his children – no one is rejected in the process as Esau and Ishmael were in previous generations. Each child, therefore, is the fulfillment of God's promise to Jacob. Each child will become the father of a tribe who will bear that child's name forever.

Jacob is satisfied because God's promise to him is being fulfilled. But Rachel wants to be a part of that process. Until Jacob, each forefather had only one wife who became a mother of Israel –

Sarah and Rebekah. And although Jacob falls in love with Rachel and chooses her to be his one wife, it is Leah whom he marries first and who first bears him children. Rachel is not merely jealous of her sister as a mother of six children. She is jealous of Leah's role as a mother of Israel. Rachel is desperate to fill that role, as well.

Eventually, Rachel's prayers are answered and she bears two sons, Joseph and Benjamin. Joseph, like Leah's son Judah, is destined for royalty. Joseph will be second to the king of Egypt, but more significantly, Joseph's descendant Jeroboam will establish the Kingdom of Israel. And even as Joseph's children are dispersed all over the world and become lost to the Jewish people, her son Benjamin remains connected with Judah and is an integral part of the Jewish people today.

But it is Rachel who, more than any other Mother of Israel, is the mother we seek and the mother who seeks us. ***"A voice is heard in Ramah, lamentation and bitter weeping. Rachel is weeping for her children; she refuses to be comforted for her children, because they are no more"*** (Jeremiah 31:14*) [Jeremiah31:15]. Rachel weeps for the children of all of Israel as they leave for exile, and God promises Rachel: ***"Keep your voice from weeping, and your eyes from tears, for there is a reward for your work... and they shall come back from the land of the enemy"*** (Jeremiah 31:15-16*) [Jeremiah 31:16-17].

Rachel wanted so much to be a mother of Israel that she did, indeed, become the quintessential mother – weeping for all the Children of Israel. To this day, women visit the grave of Rachel, located in Bethlehem, to pray for fertility. As they pray to God they ask Him to remember their mother Rachel and to bless them with children of their own.

---

* Jeremiah 31:15-17 is Jeremiah 31:14-16 in the Jewish Bible which includes the same text but a slightly different numbering in some places.

But his sons were with his livestock in the field.

A teenager cares for his sheep near Talmon

Vayishlach

Genesis 32:4 – 36:43

Jacob is torn between two values – the desire to live in peace and be accepted by the local inhabitants, and the desire to defend the honor of his daughter and of his family.

This week's portion tells of Jacob's return to the Land of Canaan, beginning with his encounter with Esau, then with the people of Shechem. The portion ends with the history of Esau and his descendants.

Jacob's encounter with the Canaanites in Shechem is troubling. On the one hand, Jacob is very careful to enter the area peacefully, and he purchases a piece of land from Hamor, the ruler of the area, and it is on this piece of land that he pitches his tents. Feeling safe in the area, Jacob's daughter Dina goes visiting with the local girls and is seized by Shechem, Hamor's son, who rapes her and holds her prisoner. Shechem then begins a process of negotiations with Jacob to marry Dina.

Jacob is strangely quiet throughout the incident: ***"Now Jacob heard that he had defiled his daughter Dina. But his sons were with his livestock in the field, so Jacob held his peace until they came"*** (Genesis 34:5).

When Jacob's sons arrive, however, they take over the conversation, bargaining with Shechem and with Hamor, ***"deceitfully"*** (Genesis 34:13). They create a massive subterfuge, convincing Shechem and Hamor that they would, indeed, consider marrying their sons and daughters but only after the Canaanites undergo circumcision. When the Canaanites have agreed and performed the operation, and when they are at their weakest, Simeon and Levi massacre the men of the city and release their sister Dina.

When the entire incident is over, Jacob is angry and says to his sons: ***"You have brought trouble on me by making me stink to the inhabitants of the land"*** (GENESIS 34:30). Simeon and Levi answer: ***"Should he treat our sister like a prostitute?"*** (GENESIS 34:31). Here the story ends, Jacob never responds.

I believe that Jacob is torn between two values in this story – the desire to live in peace and be accepted by the local inhabitants, and the desire to defend the honor of his daughter and of his family. He is similarly conflicted in his encounter with Esau. He wants to appease Esau in order to enter the Land of Israel in peace, and in response to Esau's request that they travel together, Jacob assures Esau that he will follow ***"his lord"*** to Seir. But he never does get there. He stops in Succot and then arrives in Shechem. Clearly, Jacob's offer to come to Seir is part of his deferential treatment of Esau, an act of appeasement and nothing more. Jacob is eager to separate himself from Esau as quickly as possible, in order to preserve his own identity as the heir of Abraham in the Land of Canaan.

Simeon and Levi are zealous indeed, and immediately respond with cunning and with force. Jacob may be fearful of negative repercussions, but there don't seem to be any. And, at the end of the day, the brothers have ensured that Abraham and Isaac's ban against intermarriage with Canaanites is preserved.

But Jacob does get the last word. Just before his death, he criticizes Simeon and Levi for their rashness and makes it clear that their way is not his: ***"Simeon and Levi are brothers; weapons of violence are their swords. Let my soul come not into their council;***

O my glory, be not joined to their company. For in their anger they killed men" (Genesis 49:5-6).

Jacob has no argument with the motivation of Dina's brothers to defend her honor, her identity as a daughter of Israel. He acted with similar motivation when he separated himself from Esau. For that reason, he does not respond to their query, ***"Should he treat our sister like a prostitute?"*** (Genesis 34:31).

But Jacob does question their methods. Not through rashness. Not through deceit and murder, if there is another way. The zealous often have justice on their side, but it is their methods, their lack of patience, their lack of caution, that create turmoil and conflict. And, sometimes, it is the silence of the reasonable that allows the zealous to prevail.

In August 2005, when close to 10,000 Jews were forced from their homes in Gush Katif, there was no violence.

A young woman weeps before being expelled from Gush Katif

Vayeshev

Genesis 37:1 – 40:23

Many wondered why the 10,000 Jews expelled from their homes in Gaza did not use weapons to defend their land. Thank God, the lesson of Joseph's sale remains strong.

This week's portion begins the story of Joseph. We learn that Jacob favors Joseph and buys him a striped coat, which results in the brothers' terrible jealousy of him. Joseph is introduced to us as a dreamer, and as he interprets his dreams, it becomes clear that he sees himself as superior to his brothers. The story progresses, or actually regresses, until the brothers plot to kill Joseph, then sell him to a caravan of traders instead. Joseph is brought to Egypt, sold as a slave and the portion ends with him in prison.

The resolution of this story will play itself out in subsequent chapters, but it is the sale of Joseph by his brothers that lies at the core of all that happens in this portion. In the middle of the portion, clearly interrupting the flow of the story, is the story of Judah and Tamar. But this story is carefully placed in order to present a different Judah, a man who has clearly strayed from righteousness, and is suffering for it. His sons have been killed by God, he visits a prostitute (or so he thinks) and is willing to have his daughter-in-law killed. Following the sale of his brother Joseph, a horrendous crime in which he played a central role, Judah is a troubled man.

The unity of the brothers is unraveling. How is it that these jealous, warring brothers will become a unified nation able to serve God and receive His commandments at Sinai? The bondage in Egypt will play a critical role in forging the nation. The Nation of Israel will not emerge from slavery a perfect nation. But they will have become a nation, and they will leave Egypt as one. Perhaps it is Pharaoh who helps this process along – for when he enslaves the Children of Israel and then decrees that all Jewish boys must be put to death, he creates a common destiny for all of the Children of Israel.

Centuries later, in the second century of the Common Era, there were 10 martyrs of Israel, scholars and rabbis who were put to death by the Romans for their insistence on maintaining their faith, teaching the Torah and keeping God's commandments. These were very righteous men and their wisdom and teachings are studied to this very day. On Yom Kippur, there is a portion of the prayer service that tells the story of these 10 martyrs and states a curious reason for their horrible suffering – the sale of Joseph by his brothers. Clearly, these 10 martyrs, living so many centuries after the sale, could not be held responsible for that event. Also, by ascribing their suffering to such a distant event, it is clear that these men were righteous and their personal deeds did not bring such a terrible fate upon them.

I can't begin to give an answer as to why these 10 men were killed. But I believe the prayer service is making a profound connection between the sale of Joseph and centuries of Jewish history. The sale of Joseph is the epitome of civil war, of sibling rivalry at its ugliest and most dangerous. The second Temple period, the last centuries before the Common Era and the first century of the Common Era, was rife with division and downright hatred within the Jewish people. Our sages consider this to be the primary reason for the destruction of the Temple.

The sale of Joseph was a terrible crime and foreshadows the worst times in our history, when Jew fought against Jew. Since the destruction of the Second Temple, the Jewish people have been united in their absolute refusal to fight against one another. We are vociferous and often argue loudly and vehemently, but we will not resort to violence or civil war.

It took centuries, but we finally did learn the lesson of the sale of Joseph. Perhaps the death of the 10 martyrs actually sealed the chapter on this issue and forever seared the idea in our collective consciousness that we will never resort to civil war. Perhaps, like the bondage in Egypt, it was the hatred directed against us as a nation that helped to solidify this consciousness.

In August 2005, when close to 10,000 Jews were forced from their homes in Gush Katif in the Gaza Strip, many wondered why the Jews of Gush Katif were not violent – did not use weapons to defend their homes and property. Thank God, the lesson of Joseph's sale remains strong.

When we reach the abyss, are we able to produce the words and the feelings necessary to bring unity and love among our people?

A family leaves their home quietly in Gush Katif *(photo: Miri Zahi)*

Miketz

Genesis 41:1 – 44:17

When we reach the abyss, are we able to produce the words and the feelings necessary to bring unity and love among our people?

In this week's Torah portion, we continue the story of Joseph in Egypt. The portion begins with Joseph's rise to power, thanks to his successful interpretation of Pharaoh's dream. He is given full responsibility for feeding the nation and, indeed surrounding nations, during the upcoming famine. It is in this position that he meets up with his brothers, those same people who had so cruelly sold him as a slave many years earlier.

In Genesis 42:7-8, we are told repeatedly that Joseph recognizes his brothers but they fail to recognize him. This is easy to understand, as he is now older, dressed as royalty, speaking Egyptian, and has attained a position that his brothers would never have expected him to fill. He also has an Egyptian name (Genesis 41:45). But Joseph recognizes his brothers and he remembers his dreams (Genesis 42:9). This is clearly a reference to one of the causes of their jealousy and hatred for him as they declared on that fateful day so many years earlier – ***"Here comes this dreamer"*** (Genesis 37:19). Joseph remembers his brothers and how they had treated him, their own flesh and blood. In the story that follows, Joseph attempts to test his brothers, their loyalty to one another and their willingness to sacrifice for each other, rather than kill one another.

Joseph is not disappointed, for clearly the brothers have learned their lesson and repented. When Joseph imprisons them all and demands that they send a representative to bring Benjamin, they refuse. They remain in custody for three days. When Joseph suggests that they surrender one brother to his custody while the rest return to Canaan to bring him Benjamin, they immediately recognize their sin against Joseph: ***"In truth we are guilty concerning our brother, in that we saw the distress of his soul, when he begged us and we did not listen. That is why this distress has come upon us"*** (GENESIS 42:21-22).

In the end, Joseph seizes Simeon and imprisons him and the rest have no choice but to leave without him. Jacob refuses to let Benjamin go. However, when the famine has deepened and they are facing starvation Reuben steps forward and takes responsibility: ***"Kill my two sons if I do not bring him back to you. Put him in my hands, and I will bring him back to you"*** (GENESIS 42:37).

Finally, when Joseph frames Benjamin by planting royal vessels in his bags, Judah stands up for Benjamin and insists on being imprisoned in his stead. Joseph sets in motion an elaborate plan to test his brothers. He must know whether they will be willing to betray their younger brother, Benjamin, son of Rachel, his own mother, or whether they have repented their ways. Only after they have passed the test will he reveal himself to them.

Interestingly, the portion ends with Genesis 44:17, just before Judah begins his moving, dramatic monologue to Joseph. The portion leaves us in great suspense – will Joseph take mercy on his brothers or will he manipulate his position to avenge what they had done to him years earlier? By cutting the portion at this point, by leaving us with this question, we recognize that Joseph could easily have taken either route. Not only are the brothers being tested, but Joseph is being tested as well. The fate of the Jewish people rests on this meeting between the brothers – will it end with tears and embraces, or in irreparable division and animosity?

We, who have read the next verses, already know the answer. But sometimes it is necessary to cut the portion at that pivotal point, so that we can test ourselves, ask ourselves the question. When we reach the abyss, are we able to bridge the gap – are we able to produce the words and the feelings necessary to bring unity and love among our people?

Jacob recalled his spiritual relationship with Joseph.

Teen-agers studying Torah in Sussya, building a spiritual relationship

Vayigash

Genesis 44:18 – 47:27

Jacob knows that this is not merely a journey to see Joseph before he dies – this is a journey that has monumental significance to the Nation of Israel.

This week's portion begins in the middle of the story of the final confrontation between Joseph and his brothers, before Joseph reveals himself to them. At the end of last week's portion, we have heard Joseph's cruel accusations and Judah's failed attempts to appease him. But in this week's portion, we see Judah rise to the occasion, as he begins the speech of his life, an amazing, emotional, passionate and factual address to the man he believes holds the power of life and death over them. I would like to focus on the verses that describe the brothers' first encounter with Jacob upon their return home and the subsequent descent to Egypt.

"And they told him: Joseph is still alive, and he is ruler over all the land of Egypt. And his heart became numb, for he did not believe them." (Genesis 45:26)

Imagine the scene – Jacob has never ceased mourning for his beloved Joseph and now he is told, all of a sudden, that Joseph is not only alive but is the ruler of Egypt. Of course, Jacob has trouble believing this news. But then the brothers fill him in on all of the details ***"and when he saw the wagons that Joseph had sent to carry him, the spirit of their father Jacob revived"*** (Genesis 45:27).

The commentaries have long questioned, what was it about the wagons that aroused his spirit and enabled him to believe that Joseph was, indeed, alive. There is an interesting Midrash that explains that Jacob and Joseph had been studying a Biblical passage together, that connected with wagons, and Jacob recalled this when he saw the wagons. There was no Bible written at this time, so this Midrash is not to be taken literally. But what it does reflect is the fact that Jacob recalled his spiritual relationship with Joseph. He understood that Joseph had in fact sent for him and that Joseph's call to him would have spiritual, and perhaps prophetic, consequences.

Immediately thereafter, Jacob decides to go to Egypt himself. His initial statement reflects an intention to visit – to see Joseph one more time before he dies (GENESIS 45:28). But the actual preparations and procession to Egypt indicate that the entire family is moving to that land for a very long time. And the journey is of prophetic proportion indeed. God appears to Jacob just before his departure from Canaan and He says to him:

"I am God, the God of your father. Do not be afraid to go down to Egypt, for there I will make you into a great nation. I myself will go down with you to Egypt, and I will also bring you up again" (GENESIS 46:3-4).

When the children of Jacob first leave Canaan to seek food in Egypt, Jacob says to them:

"Go down and buy grain for us there, that we may live and not die. So ten of Joseph's brothers went down to buy grain in Egypt" (GENESIS 42:2-3).

The journey to Egypt is consistently referred to as a descent, as a going down to Egypt. While it is customary to refer to the trip from Israel to Egypt as a descent (GENESIS 12:10), there seems to be something far more powerful at work here. Rashi, the classic

Jewish commentator notes that the Hebrew word that Jacob uses for *"go down"* (Redu) is the numerical equivalent of 210 – the number of years that the Children of Israel are actually enslaved in Egypt. When Jacob instructed his children to go to Egypt, there is a foreboding of the long exile this original journey will set in motion.

That foreboding is present even more so in the final journey of Jacob and his children to Egypt, and implicit in God's promise to Jacob are the dangers and long exile that they will endure throughout the centuries. Two generations earlier, God had warned Abraham that his children would be strangers in a strange land and that they would be enslaved there (Genesis 15:13). This Divine warning had probably been preserved as a family tradition and Jacob would have sensed that his journey would be the start of that long exile. But Jacob also knows that he has no choice – this is not merely a journey to see Joseph before he dies – this is a journey that has monumental significance to the Nation of Israel. Joseph has beckoned to him on a spiritual level as well.

"They also took their livestock and their goods, which they had gained in the land of Canaan, and came into Egypt, Jacob and all his offspring with him, his sons, and his sons' sons with him, his daughters, and his sons' daughters. All his offspring he brought with him into Egypt" (Genesis 46:6-7).

They leave the Land of Canaan as Jacob's family and will only return after becoming the Nation of Israel, to a land that will be forever known as the Land of Israel.

It is this clinging to the land that stands out in Jacob's final messages to his children.

Working the land in Bet Hagai

Vayechi

Genesis 47:28 – 50:26

It is this devotion to the land as the concrete expression of a faith in God's promises to His people that has kept the people of Israel together, strong and faithful for centuries.

In this week's portion, we finish the book of Genesis with the conclusion of the story of Joseph and his brothers – the brothers and Jacob are all in Egypt, Jacob blesses his children before his death and the book closes with the death of Joseph.

Before his death and before he gathers all of his children for his final words, Jacob calls Joseph separately and asks for his promise to bury him in the Land of Canaan. Later, when he has gathered all of his sons, Jacob commands his children to bury him in the land of his forefathers:

"Then he commanded them and said to them, Bury me with my fathers in the cave that is in the field of Ephron the Hittite, in the cave that is in the field at Machpelah, to the east of Mamre, in the land of Canaan, which Abraham bought with the field from Ephron the Hittite to possess as a burying place. There they buried Abraham and Sarah his wife. There they buried Isaac and Rebekah his wife, and there I buried Leah." (Genesis 49:29-31)

In an earlier conversation with Joseph, Jacob mentions, almost by way of apology, that he was unable to bury Rachel, Joseph's mother, there, for she had died along the way (Genesis 48:7).

It is almost as if Jacob has to have this conversation with Joseph before he mentions the burial of Leah in the Machpela cave to all of his sons.

What struck me though is the level of detail that Jacob uses to describe the Machpela cave. Clearly, this is a location that is well known in the family, for each of the forefathers and foremothers are buried there. In any case, mentioning the cave of Machpela in Mamre should have been enough to identify the place. And yet, Jacob recites the history of the place, the fact that Abraham purchased it from Ephron and the list of each of the family members who are buried there.

Later, after Jacob's death, the funeral procession is described in detail and again, the identification of the place of burial mentions that the cave was purchased by Abraham (Genesis 50:13). And there was similar detail when Abraham actually purchased the cave. Each part of the negotiation is set forth, and over and over again it is mentioned that Abraham has purchased the cave. (Genesis 23)

The detail mentioned here is not for the understanding of the children of Jacob. It is for the understanding of the generations who will read this account in later years. Today, the nations of the world do not recognize that Hebron is a Jewish city. Even some of the Jews in Israel have trouble recognizing our claim to the city and question whether a house legally purchased by Jews in Hebron, just a few hundred meters from the Cave of Machpela, can be occupied by Jews.

But beyond the detail and the repetition, we cannot lose sight of the fact that Jacob insists on being buried in Hebron. It is his most important testament to his children and, in fact, Joseph obtains permission from Pharaoh to leave Egypt because of his pledge to his father. And before Jacob even left for Egypt, God promises him he would return to the land, although not necessarily in his lifetime (Genesis 46:4). Clearly, this promise, more than anything, calms Jacob and reassures him.

The Land of Israel is the land promised to our forefathers. Although these great men wandered through the land, and Abraham and Jacob both left the land for periods of time, they were all buried in the land. Each of the forefathers returned to their source, to the land that God had promised to them and to their children ever after.

For centuries, there were Jews who would try to make it to the Land of Israel before they died, to be buried there if nothing else. Jews outside of Israel are often buried with a bit of dirt from the Land of Israel thrown into the grave. And many Jews today living outside of Israel arrange to be buried in Israel. Perhaps it is the contact with eternity that is entwined with death, that pulls Jews back to the Land of their fathers, the land where Abraham bought a burial cave for his wife Sarah, a cave that has remained at the center of our national identity ever since.

It is this clinging to the land that stands out in Jacob's final messages to his children. And it is this devotion to the land as the concrete expression of a faith in God's promises to His people that has kept the people of Israel together, strong and faithful for centuries.

As we continue to build homes, we follow this same message, continue doing what we can and trust God to save us.

Building new homes in Maskiot

SHEMOT

EXODUS 1:1 – 6:1

As we continue to build homes and deepen our roots in Judea and Samaria, we follow this same message and continue doing what we can and trust God to save us.

The first portion of the Book of Exodus is one of transformation – the children of Israel, the family of Jacob, become the ***"Hebrews"*** and the Children of Israel, with a national focus. The family of Amram and Yocheved become the first family of Israel, as Moses is transformed from infant, to impulsive young man, to leader and prophet. The process of transformation in each case is both moving and beautiful.

I would like to focus my thoughts on Miriam, Moses' sister who watches carefully as the Daughter of Pharaoh reaches out to draw Moses from the water. She is a young girl but she has great concern for the fate of her baby brother. As Pharaoh's daughter takes pity on the child and decides to care for him, Miriam is there, on the spot, to suggest her own mother as a wet-nurse for the new baby. ***"So the girl went and called the child's mother"*** (EXODUS 2:8).

Later on in the Bible, we learn more about Miriam. We learn that she is a leader and initiator, as she leads the women in song and dance after the parting of the Red Sea. ***"And Miriam chanted for them: Sing to the Lord, for He has triumphed gloriously, horse and driver He has hurled into the sea"*** (EXODUS 15:21).

And we learn that Miriam is an outspoken woman and she is punished by God with leprosy when she gossips about her brother's wife. And when she dies, she is mourned by the entire nation.

The Midrash tells a fascinating story about Miriam that adds an additional dimension to her character, but is quite consistent with the qualities we already see in the Biblical story. After Pharaoh decrees the death of all Jewish babies, insisting that they be thrown mercilessly into the Nile, the Midrash tells us that many men separated from their wives, so as not to risk pregnancy and the birth of a baby that would then be slaughtered by Pharaoh. Amram and Yocheved separated as well. However, Miriam with a wisdom and poignancy far exceeding her years, scolds her father and insists that her parents come back together. She tells them: isn't it enough that Pharaoh has decreed death to the sons of Israel – by separating, you are decreeing death on both the sons and daughters of Israel! Moved by their daughter's anguish, Amram and Yocheved reunite and the result is the birth of Moses.

The message of this tale is indeed powerful and it is this message that has resonated to Jewish students for centuries. Amram and Yocheved tried to avoid what they perceived as certain tragedy, by ensuring that no future children would be born in their family. But they did not take into account God's role in the situation. Miriam essentially told her parents that if God wanted their child to survive, the child would be a girl. What Miriam and her parents could not envision is that the son that would be born from their union would actually save the Jewish people and be God's own messenger to them.

It was not for Amram and Yocheved to try and outsmart the decree, nor outsmart God. It was for them to continue doing what they knew was right, and to rely on God to bring salvation. As we continue to build homes and deepen our roots in Judea and Samaria, despite the various peace plans that are placed on and off the table, we follow this same message. It is not for us to stop building in order to avoid having our homes destroyed. We must continue doing what we can and trust God to save us. And if our houses are destroyed, we will have to accept it as God's will.

The right of the Jewish people to the Land of Israel is about our roots in the land.

The Lone Oak Tree in Gush Etzion, a symbol of the determination of the survivors of Kfar Etzion to return home

VAERA

EXODUS 6:2 – 9:35

These incredible spiritual giants are ready for redemption and are helping others to seek their faith and reach out to God.

This week's portion begins with Exodus 6:2. God speaks to Moses and explains to him that He is the God who appeared to Abraham, Isaac and Jacob, that He hears the suffering of the Children of Israel and that He will keep His promise with their forefathers and free them from the bondage of Egypt.

"Moses spoke thus to the people of Israel, but they did not listen to Moses, because of their broken spirit and harsh slavery." (EXODUS 6:9)

This exchange between God and Moses and the subsequent repetition of the message to the Children of Israel, contains a powerful message to us, the Children of Israel, even today. God establishes the moral basis for the redemption of the Children of Israel – based on the covenant that He made with our forefathers ***"to give them the land of Canaan, the land in which they lived as sojourners"*** (EXODUS 6:4). Not only did God promise the land to our forefathers, but the fact that our forefathers actually dwelled in the land already, seems to give that promise extra significance. The right of the Jewish people to the Land of Israel is not only a question of God's promise; it is a question of our roots in the land.

During this passage, there are five phrases that represent redemption: ***"I will bring you out"***, ***"I will deliver you"***, ***"I will***

redeem you", ***"I will take you"***, and finally, ***"I will bring you into the land..."*** (EXODUS 6:6-8). At the Passover Seder, when we celebrate the redemption from Egypt, we drink four cups of wine. The number four is said to represent the four different phrases that represent redemption – the first four mentioned in these passages. But what of the fifth phrase – ***"And I will bring you to the land?"***

Throughout our history, Jews have remembered the redemption from Egypt not only as a significant historical event but as one that would continue to be significant for centuries. Even during the worst of our persecution in strange lands, we knew that God had chosen us and had rescued us from our first persecutor, the wicked Pharaoh. But we were in exile, not in the Land of Israel, so we did not celebrate the final phase of redemption, at least not in the same way as we celebrated the first four.

There is a fifth cup of wine at the Seder table, however, one that is placed in the center of the table and is not drunk by anyone. It is designated for Elijah the prophet, the man who will return one day to herald the arrival of the Messiah (MALACHI 3:23*) [MALACHI 4:5-6] It is this language of redemption that refers to the return to the Land of Israel that is intimately connected to the arrival of the Messiah, and, therefore, it is this cup of wine, that we don't yet drink.

Gadi Taub, a secular Israeli, wrote a book (in Hebrew) entitled, ***"The Settlers"***. The book is the author's attempt to understand our movement. He demonstrates some understanding of our motivation, but his main criticism is aimed at the fact that the ***"settlers"*** perceive modern Zionist and Israeli events as involving redemption or the beginning of a Messianic age. But for a religious person who believes in the truth of the Scriptures, is there really any alternative vision? For centuries, as we gathered around the

---

* Malachi 4:1-6 is Malachi 3:19–24 in the Jewish Bible

Passover Seder, we filled the Cup of Elijah and prayed that he would come and herald the coming of Messiah. We understood that Messiah's coming was intimately connected with our return to the Land of Israel. If we are now returning to the Land of Israel, like never before in our history, and we have even been privileged to return to the heart of the Land, to Judea and Samaria, how can we not invoke that fifth phrase of redemption, mentioned in this weeks portion: ***"I will bring you into the land that I swore to give to Abraham, to Isaac, and to Jacob. I will give it to you for a possession. I am the Lord"*** (EXODUS 6:8).

This then is the culmination of the redemption promised by God to Moses and the Children of Israel in Egypt, so many years ago. And this then is the culmination of the redemption that we are now experiencing and that God will continue to unfold before our very eyes.

Many around the world and in our own country are like the Children of Israel – they are unable to listen to Moses because of their ***"broken spirit"*** and hard work. They miss the greater picture, and therefore, lack the faith they need to be encouraged. Thank God, there is an alternative voice gaining prominence in our country. During the war in Gaza in early 2009, every day there were Orthodox Jews, religious Zionists, interviewed on television. They were primarily parents of wounded or fallen soldiers and despite their obvious pain and suffering, expressed over and over again their faith in God and their confidence that our battle for Israel is a battle blessed by God and inspired by Him. Their faith was an inspiration for many and their words were replayed over and over, hosted by a secular media, which is usually uncomfortable with such sentiments. Unlike the Children of Israel, these incredible spiritual giants are ready for redemption and are helping others to seek their faith and reach out to God.

The dates of the Biblical holidays were set firmly in the Bible based on lunar cycles.

A full moon over Jerusalem

Bo

Exodus 10:1 – 13:16

When we celebrate the renewal of the moon that signifies the beginning of the month, it is a special day of prayers and we remember God's loving instruction to Moses.

This week's Torah portion includes the final three plagues and the beginning of the Exodus. It also includes the instructions for the celebration of the Passover holiday and the procedure for the sacrifice of the lamb. The chapter which includes these instructions, Chapter 12, begins with the following Scripture:

> ***"This month shall be for you the beginning of months. It shall be the first month of the year for you."*** (Exodus 12:2)

This is God's instruction to Moses regarding the Biblical calendar, which is a lunar calendar, and forms the basis for the Jewish method of counting months and calculating the holidays.

Rashi, the most widely-read traditional Biblical commentary, notes that the use of the words ***"this month"*** indicates that God actually pointed out the moon, the word ***"month"*** being interchangeable with the word ***"moon."*** In other words, God spoke to Moses on the first day of the lunar month and showed him the moon as it looks on the first day of the month – a tiny sliver. In this way, God instructed Moses how to identify the first day of the new month. Interestingly, the first month of the Jewish calendar is the month of Passover, the month of our redemption from slavery. In Biblical terms, it is referred to as the first month. Today, we call the month by name – Nissan.

The Bible refers to the months by number. The first time the months are referred to in the Bible is during the story of the flood, when the Bible clearly tells us the date that the waters receded (GENESIS 8:4). However, it is not until the above-quoted verse in Exodus that we understand that the first month is the Passover month, the month of Nissan. We also know (FROM DEUTERONOMY 16:1): ***"Observe the month of spring,*** *" that this month of Nissan always falls in the spring. This last verse also teaches us that we must add an extra month every 3 years (approximately) to ensure that the month of Nissan always falls in the spring, as the lunar calendar is 11 days shorter than the solar calendar.

After the destruction of the first Temple, when the Jews were exiled to Babylonia, which soon after became part of the Persian Empire, we adopted the Persian names for the months, as the Persians also used the lunar calendar. Hence the renaming of the first month, Nissan.

The dates of the Biblical holidays were set firmly in the Bible. It was, therefore, imperative, that every Jew know the exact day that the new month began so as to be able to celebrate each holiday on the right day. Also, when God actually pointed out the moon to Moses and instructed him in determining the first day of the month, He effectively handed over the authority for setting the Jewish calendar to Moses and to those spiritual leaders who would follow him. In fact, the high court of Jerusalem was solely responsible for determining the first of the month and they employed people whose job it was to look for the first moon and to report their find back to the court.

---

* The Standard English Translation uses a transliteration of the Hebrew ***"Abib"*** rather than the actual translation of the word, which is spring.

Amazingly, there was an elaborate system to ensure that the Jews throughout the Land of Israel and abroad would receive immediate word of the start of the new month. A number of mountaintops were selected that stand out from the landscape. As soon as the high court declared the new month, bonfires were lit in the hills of Judea and from there, each succeeding mountaintop boasted its own bonfire and the signal spread throughout the land and eastward towards Babylon. Two mountains that we can identify today as having participated in this ceremony are the Mt. of Olives in Jerusalem and the Sartaba Mountain in the Jordan Valley.

After the destruction of the Second Temple, these same mountains and their bonfires were used to pass signals during the Bar Kochba rebellion (in the years 132-135), the last attempt to assert Jewish sovereignty in the Land of Israel before the establishment of the State of Israel in 1948.

The first day of the month is called Rosh Chodesh in Hebrew, literally, ***"Head of the Month"***, a variation of the term used in Exodus 12 when referring to the first month. The translation quoted above refers to the ***"beginning of the months"*** but the more literal translation of ***"rosh"*** is head and indeed, the original Hebrew uses the word ***"Rosh."*** To this very day, it is a special day when special prayers of praise are sung to God. And each month, when we celebrate the renewal of the moon that signifies the beginning of the month, we remember God's loving instruction to Moses: ***"This month."***

And one more thought – God also uses the term ***"this"*** when he promises Abraham the Land of Israel – ***"To your offspring I will give this land"*** (Genesis 12:7). The intimacy of God's instruction to both Abraham and Moses is truly awe-inspiring!

The transformation from a nation of slaves to a nation of fighters is amazing.

Maintaining a safe presence in Alon

Beshalach

Exodus 13:17 – 17:16

The transformation from a nation of slaves who are miraculously rescued from the Egyptian army, to a nation of fighters who can stand up to Amalek is amazing.

This week's Torah portion begins with the Exodus of the Children of Israel from Egypt and ends with the war against Amalek. And war is a theme that runs through this week's portion in a very interesting way. The portion begins with an explanation of the road chosen to leave Egypt:

"When Pharaoh let the people go, God did not lead them by way of the land of the Philistines, although that was near. For God said, Lest the people change their minds when they see war and return to Egypt." (Exodus 13:17)

As the Children of Israel approach the Red Sea, God promises victory and salvation with these words: ***"The Lord will fight for you, and you have only to be silent"*** (Exodus 14:14). And indeed, God does battle with the Egyptians as the Children of Israel look on. It is a miraculous victory indeed. The Red Sea splits and enables the entire camp of Israel to pass through with ease, unharmed. Just after they cross the sea, the waters return to their normal status and the Egyptians, the entire army, eager as they are to chase the Israelites, are caught up in the sea and drowned. An astounding victory indeed!

The two verses quoted above encompass two different sorts of battles – a physical battle between nations and a miraculous battle waged by God alone, harnessing the forces of nature to defeat an enemy as mortal human beings stand by and watch. God knew that the Nation of Israel in their downtrodden state, still with a slave mentality, would not be able to face an all-out war with the Philistines. Clearly, God would have stood by Israel's side and ensured their victory, but the victory would have also depended on the will of the Israelites to fight, and their ability to plan strategies and persist until the enemy was defeated. The Children of Israel were not ready for this sort of battle when they left Egypt and therefore, God wrought his own personal battle against the Egyptians.

At the end of the portion, however, we read about the attack of the Amalekites against the Israelites, while they are still weak and newly released from slavery. The Bible lashes out against the Amalekites for daring to war against Israel during such a vulnerable period and just after God had so clearly demonstrated He was Israel's protector. The Children of Israel are commanded to destroy every remnant of Amalek upon entry into the Land. (DEUTERONOMY 25:17-19)

But the Children of Israel actually do battle against Amalek and they prevail. The battle is an interesting one, indeed. On the one hand, Joshua is a general – he forms an army and leads the Israelites into battle. On the other hand, Moses raises his hands as a sign of faith in God and of confidence in His deliverance of Israel in this battle. The combination of a faith-based gesture and actual fighting wins the day and the Amalekites are defeated. ***"For God has waged war against Amalek who has dared to come up against Him."*** (EXODUS 17:16)

The transformation from a nation of slaves who are miraculously rescued from the Egyptian army, to a nation of fighters who can stand up to Amalek is amazing, and it is the parting of the Red Sea which actually sets the stage for the transformation. The Children of Israel witnessed God's victory over their former masters. This not only demonstrated the power of God but also brought about the total defeat of those who had held them as slaves. As a result, they are able to begin the process of leaving their slave mentality behind.

Furthermore, they sing the Song of the Sea – the beautiful song of praise to God which Moses and the Children of Israel sing just after the defeat of the Egyptians. Perhaps it is the actual song, that combination of powerful words and music, that acts as a catharsis for the Children of Israel, enabling them to express their immense gratitude to God and, at the same time, enabling them to internalize the fact that God is with them, that God will indeed protect them against whatever dangers come upon them in the future. And it is this internalization of faith and reliance upon God that enables them to fight Amalek.

Jethro is not a member of the Children of Israel, but his acceptance of God enables him to be allied with them.

Christians volunteer in the vineyards of Samaria *(photo: HaYovel)*

YITRO

EXODUS 18:1 – 20:23

Jethro is not a member of the Children of Israel, but his independent recognition of God's greatness is the basis for an alliance that withstands the generations.

This week's portion begins with Jethro's historic visit to the Children of Israel in the desert. The story begins in Exodus: ***"Jethro, the priest of Midian, Moses' father-in-law, heard of all that God had done for Moses and for Israel his people, how the Lord had brought Israel out of Egypt."*** (EXODUS 18:1)

This verse is packed with information that tells us a great deal about Jethro and about his motivation to join his son-in-law in the desert.

Jethro is a high priest of Midian. He is not only a member of a pagan nation but is a religious leader. We have previously met Jethro as Moses' father-in-law, but Scripture reminds us of this fact anyway, perhaps to contrast the religious leader of the Midianites with the religious leader of the Israelites. Not only are these two men of great stature in opposing religions, but they are family, and they clearly respect one another greatly.

Jethro is spurred on to join Moses because of what he has heard about the miracles that God performed in taking the Children of Israel out of Egypt. Presumably, he has heard of the 10 plagues, of the parting of the Red Sea, and of the total defeat of the powerful Egyptian army as it attempted to attack a rag-tag group of former slaves, men, women and children -

"We will go with our young and our old. We will go with our sons and daughters and with our flocks and herds." (EXODUS 10:9)

And immediately following that miraculous event, the Children of Israel are attacked by Amalek, a powerful band of nomadic tribes, and roundly defeat them. Jethro joins Moses because he wants to know more.

When Jethro hears the entire sequence of events as told to him by Moses, he responds:

"Blessed be the Lord who has delivered you out of the hand of the Egyptians and out of the hand of Pharaoh and has delivered the people from under the hand of the Egyptians. Now I know that the Lord is greater than all gods." (EXODUS 18:10-11)

Jethro, a priest of a pagan religion, recognizes and declares publicly that his faith was wrong – that the God of Israel is all powerful and should be worshipped and obeyed.

From this moment on, Jethro ties his fate, in one form or another, to the Jewish people. He remains a separate family, but closely allied to and neighbors with Israel. It is not clear whether Jethro remains with the Children of Israel and enters the Land of Israel with them or not. Exodus 18:27 indicates that Jethro returns home. But Numbers 10:29 finds his father-in-law back with them and the discussion arises once again whether Jethro will leave. Scripture never says what Jethro decides to do. (In this verse, Jethro is referred to as Hobab, one of several names for the same person, identified always as Moses' father-in-law.) However, in the Book of Judges, we find Jethro's family leaving the City of Palms (Jericho) to join Judah in the Negev (JUDGES 1:16). And just a few chapters later, Yael, from the same family, drives the final stake into Sissra's skull, enabling the defeat of the Canaanites (Judges 4).

Later on, in the book of Samuel, we find that this same family lives near the Amalekites, and Saul is careful not to harm them while fighting the enemy Amalek. (1 Samuel 15:6)

Jethro is not a member of the Children of Israel, but his acceptance of God enables him to be allied with them, to live among them and to offer and receive help from one another. Jethro's independent recognition of God's greatness is the basis for an alliance that withstands the generations. Oh that our current neighbors would recognize God's greatness, His promises to Israel and His Torah.

God brings us back down to earth.

A Child Enjoys the Playground in Sussya

Mishpatim

Exodus 21:1 – 24:18

Life is supposed to be a constant tension and synthesis between our relationship with God and our relationship with our fellow human beings.

Most of this week's Torah portion involves various civil laws which help govern a kind and generous society. The portion begins with the laws of slavery, which when compared to the norms of society in Biblical times, are particularly humane. It continues to deal with issues of accidental killing, murder, kidnapping, respecting one's parents, personal injury and property damage issues and the relevant compensation, theft, and the just treatment of strangers, widows and orphans. Rules of justice and prohibitions against bribery are also mentioned.

These laws are presented just after the Ten Commandments are given on Mt. Sinai. Following an event of such spiritual magnitude, an event that includes thunder and lightening, trumpets blowing and God's revelation to human beings, the Torah immediately transitions to the most mundane of issues, issues regarding daily problems between human beings, with seemingly no relationship to God.

Furthermore, it is unclear when these laws were actually spoken to Moses. Just after the Ten Commandments are given,

Scripture tells us that Moses goes into the mist ***"where God was"*** (EXODUS 20:18*) [EXODUS 20:21]. God speaks to Moses and gives him these laws. However, just after Moses teaches these laws, God speaks to him and commands him to ascend the mountain to receive the tablets. The portion ends when Moses is on the mountain for 40 days and 40 nights. Does Moses go up the mountain twice, speak to God on two different occasions, or is this all one long teaching from God which Moses hears on Sinai and transmits to the Children of Israel later on? Scripture is unclear.

However, what is clear is that these basic moral and civil laws are placed in the Bible just after the Ten Commandments are given. And perhaps that is the point. It is probable that Moses actually heard these laws while on Sinai during his 40 day sojourn there, and that he actually only taught the Children of Israel these laws much later, after the sin of the Golden Calf and after Moses' final descent from Sinai. However, the Bible is communicating an important message to us by setting the order as it does.

Many faiths contain elements of spirituality, of some sort of spiritual encounter. And, it is quite natural that following such an experience, a human being will no longer be interested in mundane and earthly issues. He wants to remain in the heavens, communicating with God and attending only to his spiritual relationship. But God brings us back down to earth.

Actually, the first commandment listed after Revelation is the instruction to build an altar, out of earth. We are told that this earth-bound altar will be a human vehicle to serve God. Following this section, God takes us to the core of human moral existence. If we ignore our fellow man, if we act unjustly, if we steal, murder,

---

* Exodus 20:21 is Exodus 20:18 in the Jewish Bible

cause injury to another, we are sinning against God. We cannot absolve ourselves of responsibilities to our fellow man merely because we have experienced the spiritual. We must immediately come back down to earth and make sure the strangers in our midst are comfortable and the widows and orphans are cared for.

The human-bound commandments are purposely placed where they will ground us in our human responsibilities. And the text purposely jumps back and forth between Moses on the mountain with God and Moses teaching the people the nitty gritty of living a moral life. For that is what our life is supposed to be – a constant tension, and constant synthesis, between our relationship with God and our relationship with our fellow human beings.

Every person is commanded to do something.

Volunteers both young and old help pack food packages for the Samaria Family Assistance Program

Trumah

Exodus 25:1 – 27:19

The basic idea behind the Tabernacle is that it is a place which enables humanity, every man, woman and child, to encounter God.

This week's Torah portion is the first of four Torah portions that discuss the building of the Tabernacle and the vessels within. The details are amazing – the exact dimensions of the building and of each vessel, the materials used for both inner and outer parts, the shapes, the designs and the exact purpose of each item. And it is these precise descriptions which have enabled artists over the years to paint beautiful pictures of the Tabernacle and its vessels, as well as to construct models of the entire Tabernacle complex. One such model is on display at Ancient Shiloh, the actual site where the Tabernacle stood in its permanent format, for 369 years, after the Children of Israel entered Israel and completed the initial conquest of the land.

The portion begins, however, with basic instructions which form the backdrop for this massive construction project. The first instruction refers to the resources for the project:

"Speak to the people of Israel, that they take for me a contribution. From every man whose heart moves him you shall receive the contribution for me." (Exodus 25:1)

Scripture then goes on to specify that the contributions will be of precious metals, beautiful fabrics, leather skins, oil, spices, and precious stones. Later on, when Scripture specifies how this commandment was fulfilled, it specifically mentions that both men and women donated items to the project, including items that had been woven by the women themselves. (Exodus 35:21 – 29)

The inclusion of everyone and the encouragement of each to donate as his heart prompts him are what make this project so special. It is not the Tabernacle of a selected few, of an elite class or wealthy few, but the Tabernacle of the people. And, as such, it is every person who is commanded to do something, to contribute in some way towards its beauty and completion.

Further on in this introductory section, is a second instruction that reveals more about the purpose of the Tabernacle:

"And let them make me a sanctuary, that I may dwell in their midst." (Exodus 25:8)

Here, the word *"Mikdash,"* is used, literally a temple, although the translation uses the word sanctuary instead. It is the same word used in Chronicles and Ezekiel when referring to the Temple in Jerusalem (Ezekiel 44:1, 1 Chronicles 22:19), although in the book of Kings, the word House of God is used instead. Indeed, the instructions listed here form the basis for the construction of the more permanent Temple in Solomon's time. The Tabernacle is a temporary, transportable structure, perfectly suited for the desert and later adapted for the more permanent Shiloh. But it is only when King David conquers Jerusalem and then purchases the threshing floor from the Jebusite that the stage is set for the construction of a temple on the place ***"that the Lord your God will choose out of all your tribes to put His name and make His habitation there"*** (Deuteronomy 12:5).

But God says something amazing about the purpose of the Temple or Tabernacle. It is not a place where God will dwell within its walls. It is a place which enables God to dwell within *"their midst,"* in the midst of the Children of Israel. The Tabernacle, then, unlike pagan places of worship, is not conceived of as a physical structure meant to provide a home on earth for a god. It is a place which facilitates the relationship between God and His children.

This is reinforced by the instructions regarding the Holy Ark. ***"And you shall put the mercy seat on the top of the ark, and in the ark you shall put the testimony that I shall give you. There I will meet with you, and from above the mercy seat, from between the two cherubim that are on the ark of the testimony"*** (EXODUS 25:21-22). The ark, with its covering and cherubim is a meeting place between Moses and God, and, in turn, enables God to communicate with His people, through Moses.

The sacrifices and rituals that take place in and around the Tabernacle are all about man meeting God. The rituals involve very physical acts, of slaughter, incense, and the lighting of the menorah. But they enable man, a very physical being, to come in contact with God who has no physical being, who has no form, and cannot be seen or felt. God would never be confined to a physical structure. But the physical structure serves man's need to meet God on this earth.

This, then, is the basic idea behind the Tabernacle and both ideas are represented in the very first verses of the Torah portion. It is a place in which all of Israel must have a share and it is a place which enables humanity, every man, woman and child, to encounter God.

The creation of the State of Israel was an occasion where God and His people meet.

Young people dance with Israeli flags to the Western Wall in celebration of the reunifcaiton of Jerusalem

Tezave

Exodus 27:20 – 30:10

The creation of the State of Israel was an occasion where God and His people meet – on the holy ground of the Land of Israel, and walk together towards Redemption.

This week's portion begins with the end of Exodus Chapter 27 and includes the instructions for Aaron and their priests in their worship roles – their clothes, the sanctification process they will go through, and some instruction regarding the altar, the incense altar and the ***"tent of meeting"***. It is the instruction with regard to this ***"tent"*** that I would like to focus on.

In discussing the regular daily sacrifice, Scripture refers to the place where it will be brought:

*"At the entrance of the '**tent of meeting**' before the Lord, where I will meet with you, to speak to you there. There I will meet with the people of Israel, and it shall be sanctified by my glory."* (Exodus 29:43-44)

I have purposely put emphasis on the words '***tent of meeting***' because it is the translation of these words that I want to discuss.

The actual Hebrew words for tent of meeting are ***"Ohel Moed."*** Ohel means tent and Moed usually means time. In fact, it is this same word that is used to introduce the festivals of God (in Leviticus 23:4): *"These are the appointed **times*** *of the Lord, the*

holy convocations, which you shall proclaim at the time appointed for them.*"** In essence, however, the word ***"moed" has been used to refer to the holidays and is interchangeable with the word for festival or feast. From the verse in Leviticus, therefore, we see that the word Moed really means time, but it is used to refer to festivals.

In the scripture in our portion, however, the word is also used to denote meeting, as the end of verse 42 and verse 43 make clear, for the words for meeting, come from the same root as moed.

Clearly, then, there is a connection between these words – meeting, time and festival. And the whole concept of ***"Ohel Moed"*** or the tent of meeting, encompasses all of these meanings.

Ohel Moed is in the Tabernacle and it is the place where God and the Jewish people meet. It is where God speaks to Moses, and it is where sacrifices are brought to God by the priests on behalf of the people of Israel. These sacrifices are brought at specified times. And the festivals occur at specified dates and times.

Meeting God, it seems, is intimately involved with time. It is not a chance meeting, but one that is determined by God, according to His time and at the place of His choosing. In fact, the word meeting itself is a word that tends to denote time, place and connectedness between two people. In this case, meeting God refers to time (at His choosing, or during the festivals), place (Tabernacle) and connectedness (meeting between God and His people.)

Interestingly, the word Moed, or festival, has also been adopted to refer to the newly created holiday of Israel Independence Day. On that holiday, we greet each other with the traditional

---

* The translation actually uses the word ***"feasts"*** here but it misses the literal translation of the word ***"moed"*** in the singular or ***"moadim"*** in the plural, which literally means times.

greeting of *"Happy Moed"* or happy holiday. Secular Jews will generally celebrate Israel Independence Day in a way that does not differ much from similar celebrations in countries all over the world, although the enormous challenges we have faced since the creation of the state creates a spirit of thanksgiving that touches even the most secular Jew. But the religious Zionist views the creation of the State of Israel as a spiritual event, the culmination of the prayers and prophecies that held the nation together for centuries.

In referring to the day as a *"moed"*, perhaps we recognize that the creation of the State of Israel was not just a happy occasion, but an occasion where God and His people meet – on the holy ground of the Land of Israel, where we walk together, God and His people, through miraculous occurrences towards the ultimate Redemption.

What an amazing thought contained in just one word!

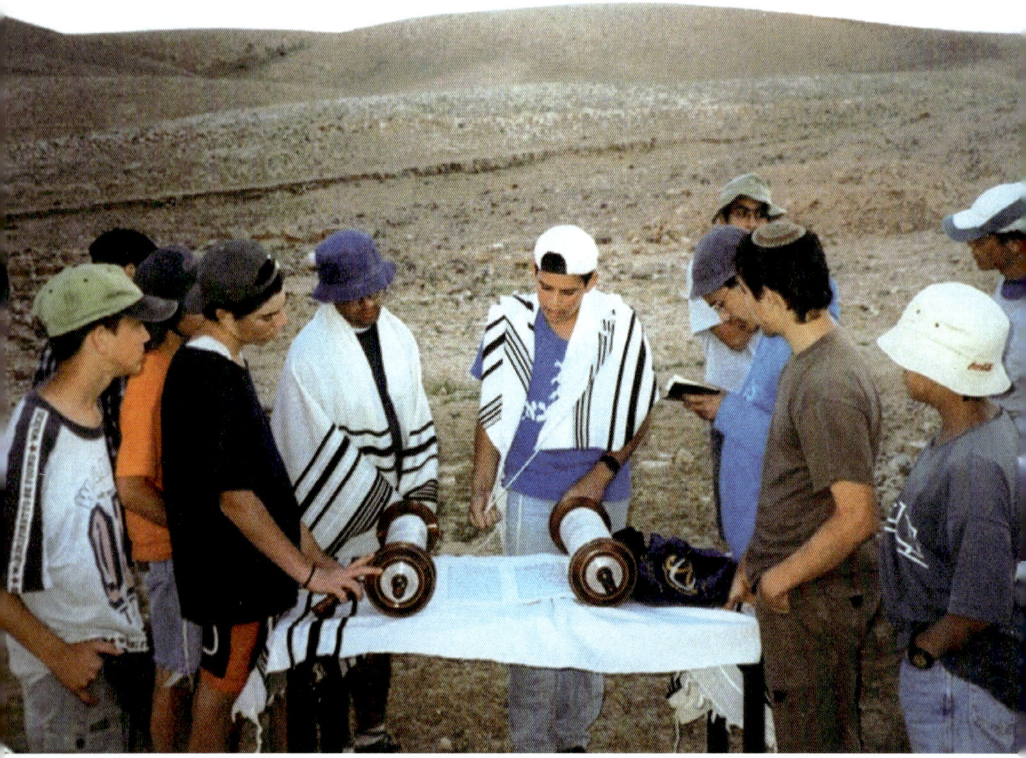

"Who is on the Lord's side? Come to me."

Sussya High School boys reading from a Torah Scroll

Ki Tisa

Exodus 30:11 – 34:35

By forcing separation between Moses and the nation, God enabled the nation to learn the vital lesson that Moses is not a god but a loyal servant.

This week's portion begins with the commandment to conduct a census among the Children of Israel through the donation of a half shekel. Other commandments follow, but the focus of the portion is the story of the Golden Calf.

It has long puzzled commentators how the Nation of Israel, just weeks after hearing God speak to them directly, after the amazing experience of Revelation at Sinai, could sin in such a drastic way. After being freed from slavery in Egypt by the one and only God of Israel, the nation slides into base idolatry, creating a golden calf which they then worship.

While it is clear that the Children of Israel had been subject to the influences of Egyptian idolatry for hundreds of years, and that clearly played a part in this incident, it is still puzzling that they would sink to such depths so soon after the experience at Sinai. A careful reading of the text, however, provides some insight.

"When the people saw that Moses delayed to come down from the mountain, the people gathered themselves together to Aaron and said to him: Up, make us gods who shall go before us. As for this

Moses, the man who brought us up out of the land of Egypt, we do not know what has become of him." (Exodus 32:1)

Moses has been gone for some weeks and the nation is getting nervous. Notice that there is no mention of God in this statement. From the nation's perspective, it is Moses who has taken them out of Egypt – God's role is missing. Furthermore, there is an implied parallel between Moses and a god who will go before them – from their perspective, Moses was a god, a wondrous individual who led them out of Egypt. If that is the case, then the absence of Moses is clearly cause for concern. Without his leadership, they would, indeed, be lost.

I don't believe that the nation actually believed Moses was a god – they knew his family, knew that he was not a supernatural being. In fact, when Moses first came to them in Egypt with God's message of imminent delivery, they rejected him and mocked him. But their relationship to him was as to a super-leader – a man with amazing powers, god-like in essence, and rather than see him as a messenger from God, with no independent powers of his own, a loyal servant of God, they saw him as akin to a god himself. They believed that Moses had the inherent power to lead them to the Promised Land.

Of course, they were wrong. It was God who had freed them from Egypt and it was God who would lead them to the Land of Israel and protect them once they got there. If something were to happen to Moses, God would provide another leader in his stead. But the nation was so dependent on Moses, that they lost their sense of perspective. Rather than see Moses as the amazing servant of God that he was, they saw him as a super hero in his own right.

God's initial response to Moses with regard to the sin of the nation reflects this idea. ***"Now therefore let me alone, that my***

wrath may burn hot against them and I may consume them, in order that I may make a great nation of you" (Exodus 32:10). God recognizes the root of the problem with the Nation of Israel – rather than a kingdom of priests and a holy nation (Exodus 19:6), dedicated to serving God, they are followers of human leaders. Therefore, God wants no part of them. He wants to create a new nation from Moses – a nation of loyal servants like Moses who follow God's word regardless of who the leader happens to be. In Moses' prayer to God begging him to continue with the Nation of Israel, he reminds God of his promise to Abraham, Isaac and Jacob, and God is pacified. Essentially, Moses says that the nation is human, that they err and will continue to err. But they are the nation of God. And when Moses returns to the people, his first statement to the nation says it all: ***"Who is on the Lord's side? Come to me."*** (Exodus 32:26). The Lord's side, not Moses' side.

Perhaps Moses' stay on Sinai was part of a vital lesson to the nation. By forcing separation between Moses and the nation, God enabled them to learn that Moses is not a god but a loyal servant. And the lesson is a vital one to us all. Leaders are often charismatic and have the power and the influence to convince people to do things they may otherwise not do. But even righteous leaders who use their power only in service of God and for the promotion of righteousness should not ever be considered a replacement for God. They are merely messengers. Blind adherence to a leader, any leader, is always dangerous.

The Tabernacle represents the very essence of human freedom and equality.

An archeological find in Shiloh, home to the Tabernacle for 369 years

Vayakhel

Exodus 35:1 – 38:20

A simple structure constructed of volunteered items easily found in ordinary households, the Tabernacle represents the very essence of human freedom and equality.

This week's Torah portion opens with Moses' instruction to the Children of Israel to donate items for the construction of the Tabernacle and its various vessels. It echoes the very similar commandment that God gave to Moses in Chapter 25. It would seem, therefore, that the repetition would be superfluous. Why didn't Scripture just tell us that Moses commanded the people to donate and they did?

In reading the verses in chapter 35, however, there is something very special that is conveyed through the details mentioned here. Like the previous instruction, Moses asks for those ***"of a generous heart"*** but he details the actual items needed for each vessel or structure: ***"Oil for the light, spices for the anointing oil and for the fragrant incense, and onyx stones and stones for setting, for the ephod and for the breast piece"*** (Exodus 35:8-9).

Moses is inspiring the people, enabling them to understand that their donation will contribute in a very direct way to a specific purpose. In the same vein, he asks for skilled craftsmen to construct very specific items: ***"The Tabernacle, its tent and its covering, its hooks and its frames, its bars, its pillars, and its bases; the ark with its poles, the mercy seat, and the veil of the screen"*** (Exodus 35:11-12).

But the most moving part is the description of the actual donations brought by the people. Again, the phrase *"everyone whose heart stirred him"* (EXODUS 35:21) is repeated.

"So they came, both men and women. All who were of a willing heart brought brooches and earrings and signet rings and armlets, all sorts of gold objects, every man dedicating an offering of gold to the Lord. And every one who possessed blue or purple or scarlet yarns or fine linen or goats' hair or tanned rams' skins or goatskins brought them. Everyone who could make a contribution of silver or bronze brought it as the Lord's contribution. And every one who possessed acacia wood of any use in the work brought it. And every skillful woman spun with her hands, and they all brought what they had spun in blue and purple and scarlet yarns and fine twined linen. All the women whose hearts stirred them to use their skill spun the goats' hair. And the leaders brought onyx stones and stones to be set, for the ephod and for the breast piece, and spices and oil for the light, and for the anointing oil, and for the fragrant incense. All the men and women, the people of Israel, whose heart moved them to bring anything for the work that the Lord had commanded by Moses to be done brought it as a freewill offering to the Lord" (EXODUS 35:22-29).

Each man and woman did what he or she could to help. Those who could spin the yarns did so. Those who had precious gems and gold and silver to donate, did so. Those who had skins or fabrics donated them. The detail presented here, of each type of donation and each person who took the time to determine how he or she could help, all as moved by their hearts, teaches a very important lesson indeed.

Often, it is the success of a project that history records. When great kings of antiquity built monuments to celebrate victories or to worship a pagan god, we know nothing of the ordinary people who participated in the construction. In fact, it is likely that these temples and monuments were built by slaves who were forced to labor with great suffering to build a magnificent structure at the whim of their master.

Not so the Tabernacle. It is a simple structure constructed of items easily found in ordinary households – fabrics and skins and jewelry. And Scripture stresses that it is built through donations, simple items brought by ordinary people, as their hearts and spirits moved them, voluntarily, to take part in the building of a structure that would serve as their center of worship, their vehicle to reach God. It is a structure that represents the very essence of human freedom and equality, even as it sets strict limits on the access of ordinary people to its innermost sanctum. But the restricted access does not reflect upon the status of the individual, for each individual is equal before God, as reflected in his ability to participate in this great national project. Restricted access is an expression of great holiness and sanctity, not of inequality and oppression. The high priest who enters the Holy of Holies represents the people and enables atonement for their sins – he serves them who have enabled this vehicle for serving God to come into existence.

When we hesitate to enter, He beckons to us.

Samaria – the land beckons to be settled by God's people

Pikudei

Exodus 38:21 – 40:38

God understands our need to feel His presence among us. And, like Moses who is reluctant to enter the Tabernacle, when we hesitate, God beckons to us.

The closing chapters of the Book of Exodus complete the section that deals with the construction of the Tabernacle. The last verses are particularly interesting.

"Then the cloud covered the Tent of Meeting, and the glory of the Lord filled the Tabernacle. And Moses was not able to enter the Tent of Meeting because the cloud settled on it, and the glory of the Lord filled the Tabernacle." (Exodus 40:34-35)

Twice, Scripture tells us that the glory of God has filled the Tabernacle, which, in essence is what the Tabernacle was for. When God first instructed Moses on this issue, He said: ***"And let them make me a sanctuary, that I may dwell in their midst"*** (Exodus 25:8).

Clearly, in having His glory fill the Tabernacle, He is dwelling among His people.

But it is this filling of the Tabernacle that prevents Moses from entering. This would seem to contradict another statement that God makes earlier regarding the purpose of the Tabernacle: ***"There I will meet with you, and from above the mercy seat, from between the two cherubim that are on the ark of the testimony, I***

will speak with you about all that I will give you in commandment for the people of Israel" (EXODUS 25:22).

If, indeed, the Tabernacle is meant for Moses to meet God and to receive His instructions there for the Children of Israel, how is it that Moses is unable to enter the Tabernacle?

There are commentaries who position Moses at the entrance of the Tabernacle or, at least, at the entrance of the inner sanctum of the Tabernacle, and that this is where God speaks to Moses. Since the word ***"tabernacle"*** refers interchangeably to the entire complex and to the inner-most sanctum, this commentary is reasonable.

The Midrash, however, provides a different perspective. Moses is a righteous man and has done exactly what God has asked him to do. God asked him to build a tabernacle and he did so, as quickly as possible. And when the Tabernacle was completed, he stood outside, in awe of God's presence, hesitant to enter the Tent of Meeting. The Midrash then quotes God as saying to Himself: ***"it is not right for Moses who constructed the Tabernacle to remain outside while I am inside. I will call to him to enter."*** Therefore, the Bible continues: ***"The Lord called Moses and spoke to him from the Tent of Meeting, saying"*** (LEVITICUS 1:1).

The Midrash weaves together the end of Exodus with the beginning of Leviticus into one cohesive story. In so doing, it portrays God as a gracious host, who recognizes Moses' important role in constructing a house for Him. And it portrays Moses as the humble and righteous servant of God who, despite having completed the building of the Tabernacle and knowing its purpose as a meeting place between God and himself, hesitates to enter the sanctuary because of his awe of God's presence. It is God, therefore, who calls to Moses and beckons to him to enter. But the Tabernacle itself represents a balance between intimacy and distance. God's presence creates awe and sets a barrier between man and God. And, indeed, it is only a few select men, like Moses, who are able to enter the inner sanctum. But when Moses does enter, he does so on behalf of all of Israel.

The essence of the Tabernacle, then, is God's calling out to man, creating an environment in which man can come close to God. The place is created, not out of man's need, or his initiative, but out of God's understanding of our need to feel His presence among us. And, like Moses, when we hesitate to enter, He beckons to us.

Every individual is responsible for his actions.

An Israeli soldier removes a Jewish family from their home in Gush Katif

Vayikra

Leviticus 1:1 – 5:26

Happy is the generation whose leadership can own up to its mistakes publicly.

The Book of Leviticus is dedicated primarily to instructing us in the various sacrifices that are brought in the Tabernacle and, later on, in the Temple, as well as other instructions pertaining to the work of the priests and the Levites. Chapter 4 begins with a discussion of the various sacrifices to be brought and procedures to be followed when someone sins accidentally, not as a result of intent but rather from carelessness or ignorance. The Torah begins with the incident of an ordained priest who makes a mistake, then moves on to the Assembly of Israel (Leviticus 4:13), which refers to the High Court, then moves on to a prince (which can refer to any political leader, such as the head of a tribe), and finally concludes with the mistakes of the individual.

Bringing a sacrifice to the Temple is a public affair – the description of the ceremony for this particular type of sacrifice is quite specific and there is nothing private about the situation. Everyone recognizes the priest or the prince and will understand, based on the type of sacrifice brought and the ceremony performed, that this leading figure has sinned. He cannot hide behind the vestments of his office, but must publicly admit that he has done something wrong, even if only by accident. Furthermore, the instruction regarding the public officials precedes the instruction for the individuals, conveying a clear message that the leadership is expected to set the standard for the nation on this issue.

Especially interesting is the passage that discusses the sacrifice brought by the High Court when the judges have ruled incorrectly (LEVITICUS 4:13-21). Imagine a Supreme Court judge who has discovered that he incorrectly interpreted his country's constitution bringing a sacrifice to atone for his incorrect ruling!

The mistake of the High Court is unique, in that it is a mistake that directly affects the people. The High Court will have issued a ruling that is later realized to be wrong, but which, in the meantime, has caused innocent people to sin and violate a commandment. In this case, then, the judges admit publicly that not only did they err but they caused others to sin as well, a weighty admission indeed.

Rashi, the 11th century Torah commentator, makes a fabulous statement regarding the first words (OF LEVITICUS 4:22): ***"That* a leader sins."***

The Hebrew word used for ***"that"*** is ***"Asher"***, which is a slightly unusual way to begin a sentence. Rashi notes the similarity between the word ***"Asher"*** and the word ***"Ashrei"*** which is the first word in Psalms 1, and means ***"Happy is"***. Rashi then states: ***"Happy is the generation whose prince makes sure to bring an atonement sacrifice for his accidental sins, even more so for his intentional sins."***

---

* The translation uses the word ***"when"*** instead of ***"that"*** which is a more accurate translation of the word *"Asher"* and highlights the difficulties in the text that Rashi is questioning.

What an amazing thought! Every individual is responsible for his actions, even those performed negligently. This is a lofty and important principle. But in so many societies, the leadership manages to escape censure. And when leaders are caught in a wrongdoing, they rarely admit their mistakes, let alone their corruption. The standard that is expected of the common man is so often ignored by the leadership – the very individuals who are expected to enforce the law and ethical standards are often lax themselves.

What a better society we would all enjoy if such were the standards of our leaders. Rashi says it best: Happy is the generation whose leadership can own up to its mistakes publicly.

Both the priests and the vessels in the Tabernacle are anointed in oil.

Olive Groves in Maskiot will provide fruit and oil for the people of Israel

Zav

Leviticus 6:1 – 8:36

With the anointing of Aaron, Moses hands over something he will never have again. He lovingly gives up a part of his leadership, so that the people can be better served.

Chapter 8 in Leviticus discusses the anointing of Aaron and his sons as priests in the Tabernacle and the anointing of the Tabernacle itself. The process is very detailed. The first step is the washing of both Aaron and his sons. Then Moses dresses Aaron. Then Moses anoints the vessels in the Tabernacle in oil. Then Moses anoints Aaron in oil. Finally, a series of sacrifices and ceremonies follow, after which Moses instructs Aaron and his sons to remain in the Tabernacle for seven days and nights. At the conclusion of this process, the Tabernacle will be ready for regular service.

A few things about this process struck me as I was reviewing the sequence. First of all, Moses is the one who takes the lead, who has received the instruction from God and who does the washing, anointing, sprinkling of the blood and so much more. Moses is the active player in this entire process – Aaron and his sons are passive recipients of their new role. Interestingly, though, Moses will not be allowed to bring the sacrifices once the Tabernacle is completed, because it is only Aaron and his sons, and his descendants forever, who are appointed to that role.

Secondly, both the priests and the vessels in the Tabernacle are anointed in oil. Generally, the anointing oil is used to appoint someone to a particular position – both Saul and David are anointed by prophets. But here, the oil is also used to anoint inanimate objects.

Lastly, when Moses instructs the priests at the end of the process, he makes it very clear that they must not leave the Tabernacle at all for 7 days ***"so that you do not die"*** (LEVITICUS 8:35). Clearly, there is a danger involved in serving God in the Tabernacle.

Each of these issues teaches us something very valuable about leadership and serving God. Until now, Moses has been the sole recipient of God's instruction and has passed that instruction on to the people. With the anointing of Aaron and his sons, however, Moses imparts some of his authority to Aaron, enabling him and his sons to be the sole people responsible for serving God in the Tabernacle. Aaron passively receives this instruction as Moses actively gives it, but Moses has actually handed over something he will never have again. He willingly and lovingly gives up a part of his leadership, so that the people can be better served, separately, by the priesthood on the one hand and by political leadership, on the other. From this point forward, there is a separation of powers and each will serve God in a totally different way.

In anointing the vessels in addition to anointing the people, Moses is designating those who will act as vessels of service to God. When the priests serve in the Temple, they do not act independently, serving God as the spirit moves them. They serve only according to His will and in accordance with His laws. They, like the vessels, are there only to serve.

And finally, the issue of danger. God has enabled us to serve Him in a Temple that is actually God's home, for it is where He is going to dwell. It is not a casual place, but a place where the utmost respect and care must be taken to obey God's will. Two chapters on, we learn of the tragic death of two of Aaron's sons after they have offered an alien fire in the Tabernacle. While it is not clear what their exact transgression was, it is clear that they have done something outside the strictures that God has laid down in the detailed specifics in the preceding chapters.

The priests spend 7 days intensely and carefully learning the procedures that they will perform once the service is turned over to them. There is no room for error. The priests are there to serve and they must do it carefully, for their very lives are at stake. It is a most serious business.

Speak to the people of Israel, saying, these are the living things that you may eat among all the animals that are on the earth.

The local petting zoo in Maale Levonah

SHMINI

LEVITICUS 9:1 – 11:47

Eating is the physical manifestation of the spiritual aspect of living a holy life and the key to understanding kosher eating is reflected in the act of distinguishing.

This week's portion contains one of the basic fundamentals of kosher eating – the list of animals that are permitted as well as a list of animals that are not. Chapter 11 begins: ***"Speak to the people of Israel, saying, these are the living things that you may eat among all the animals that are on the earth"*** (LEVITICUS 11:2-3).

This introductory statement emphasizes two issues. Firstly, the commandments for restricted eating are given solely to the Children of Israel. Secondly, there is a selection going on here – God mentions all of the animals of the earth, in a positive sense. They are, indeed, all of his creations. But He does distinguish those animals ***"among all the animals that are on the earth"*** which are permissible to the Children of Israel.

The final injunction refers to reptilian creatures which are totally forbidden, and the language here is quite extreme.

"You shall not make yourselves detestable with any swarming thing that swarms, and you shall not defile yourselves with them, and become unclean through them." (LEVITICUS 11:43)

Just the imagery of the swarming, combined with such words as detestable and defile, are enough to convey the strong message that these creatures are not to be eaten under any circumstances.

Following this verse are further injunctions against eating reptiles coupled with the injunction to be holy and sanctified: ***"for I am holy... For I am the Lord who brought you up out of the land of Egypt to be your God. You shall therefore be holy, for I am holy"*** (LEVITICUS 11:44-45).

And, finally, the summary verses of this chapter: ***"This is the law about beast and bird and every living creature that moves through the waters and every creature that swarms on the ground, to make a distinction between the unclean and the clean and between the living creature that may be eaten and the living creature that may not be eaten."*** (LEVITICUS 11:46-47)

The entire issue of Kosher eating, therefore, is an issue that involves holiness and purity and that is about distinguishing. God draws a clear parallel between obeying the kosher laws and sustaining a status of holiness, of being holy as God is holy, or, in other words, in coming as close as we can to God. This theme of being holy because God is holy, or the need to ***"imitate God"*** is repeated throughout Scripture, most notably (IN LEVITICUS 19:2): ***"You shall be holy, for I the Lord your God am holy."***

Pure eating, therefore, is part and parcel of pureness of spirit. It is the physical manifestation of the spiritual aspect of living a holy life. God assigns a detestable characteristic to reptiles as well as to other impure animals as a way of separating them from other animals which are considered pure. But these are all God's creatures. The creatures themselves are not ***"bad"*** and there is no ultimate ***"badness"*** associated with them. They are merely impure for us, for the Jewish people: ***"You shall not eat any of their flesh... they are unclean to you"*** (LEVITICUS 11:8).

They are impure for the Children of Israel, not inherently impure.

I believe that the key to understanding this issue is the final aspect of kosher eating as reflected in this chapter – the act of distinguishing. The Children of Israel are forced to distinguish between those animals which are kosher and those which are not. Perhaps the entire point of these laws is the act of distinguishing itself. God requires us to separate between things we eat and things we don't. He requires us to distinguish between the pure and impure. And, in handing these requirements only to the Children of Israel, He is requiring us to distinguish ourselves from the other nations.

There is a famous line in the classic film, ***"Fiddler on the Roof"*** where Tevye says to God something to the effect: ***"I know you have chosen us but perhaps sometimes you can choose someone else?!"*** In Tevye's case, he is complaining about the most recent misfortune which has befallen him, and the film gives an excellent portrayal of the anti-Semitism faced by the Jews of Russia during the early years of the 20th century. But this is not just a scene in a movie – it is an accurate description of the condition of the Jewish people throughout history. Yes, we have been chosen by God, for extra commandments, for extra responsibilities. But that ***"chosenness"*** has also set us apart from the other nations and has often become the source of anti-Semitism and persecution.

Far be it for me to begin to understand why God chose us. But chose us He did. And with that choice comes enormous responsibility to live a holy life, to the best of our ability, to follow God's commandments and to come as close as we can to the holiness that represents God.

The rules of purity and impurity enable us to deepen our understanding of the overwhelming power of life and the overarching value that the Bible ascribes to it.

A circumsicion ceremony funded by the Ezra Fund in Sussya

Tazria

Leviticus 12:1 – 13:59

The rules of purity and impurity enable us to deepen our understanding of the overwhelming power of life and the overarching value that the Bible ascribes to it.

This week's portion continues the discussion of ritual purity. In last week's portion, the instructions regarding purity revolved around various animals that are considered pure or impure. Those animals which are impure may never be eaten nor used for sacrifice. In this week's portion, however, the instructions revolve around situations where a person will become impure through a most natural circumstance, situations that involve illness, infection, skin problems, giving birth, and menstruation. In these cases, a person is not to avoid the situation that created the impurity, but must recognize the state and then take whatever steps are necessary to become pure once more. Until the individual is pure, he is prevented from approaching the Tabernacle or Temple and offering sacrifices to God.

The most serious type of impurity, however, is created as a result of coming into contact with a dead body. This impurity is actually discussed in other portions, but it is important to mention it in order to obtain a better understanding of the types of impurity mentioned in this week's portion. In Numbers 19, God instructs the Children of Israel how to become pure after coming into contact with a dead body. Unlike the other types of impurity, only the ashes of a red heifer can bring the individual who has come into contact with a dead body to purity. Clearly, however, ordinary individuals are not supposed to refrain from contact with a dead body. The only restriction on coming into contact with a dead body is imposed on the priests, the sons of Aaron. In Leviticus 21, God specifically instructs Aaron and his children not to come into contact with any dead body, with the exception of their immediate relatives. And the high priest is prevented from coming into contact with the remains of his closest relatives as well. From this, we learn that the impurity associated with death is the greatest impurity of all. In Jewish tradition, it is referred to as the ***"granddaddy of all impurities."***

Many commentaries, therefore, have looked for similarities between the impurity resulting from death and the other impurities mentioned in the chapters we are reading this week. To what extent do the causes of impurity mentioned in this portion relate to death?

In both menstruation and childbirth, there is an element of death, as strange as that may sound. When a woman menstruates, it signifies that she is not pregnant, that the ovum that she carried in her body was not fertilized, did not become a fetus, which would then become a child, and therefore a ***"mini-death"*** has occurred. Of course, there is no fault attributed to the woman, and women, naturally, spend many years of their lives menstruating and not becoming pregnant. But it is a small reminder that women have that incredible potential to create life and when that potential is not realized, it bears a small relationship to death. Hence the status of impurity.

A similar process occurs in childbirth. Although childbirth is the exact opposite of death – a new life enters this universe, as opposed to a life departing – as the child leaves the woman's body, there is a separation that the woman experiences from something that was life within her. And, although the life being born is cause for incredible happiness, there is a small element in this situation that includes a separation from life. Many women who have given birth, will attest to this duality of feeling – the ***"high"*** that is unparalleled by any other experience in life as a new life is born, coupled with the slight sense of ***"down"*** that the pregnancy is over. Some ascribe this to post-partum blues and hormonal changes, but perhaps there is a spiritual element present as well.

When seen from this perspective, the rules of purity and impurity contained in this portion enable us to deepen our understanding of the overwhelming power of life and the overarching value that the Bible ascribes to it. Life is from God. Life is pure. And while death is natural and expected, because it represents the negation of life, it creates a status of impurity which, temporarily, distances us from God. For God is Life.

As men and women created in God's image, we are commanded to love our neighbor as ourselves and to treat everyone with respect.

Activities at the Senior Citizens Center in Kedumim

Mezora

Leviticus 14:1 – 15:33

As men and women created in God's image, we are commanded to love our neighbor as ourselves and to treat everyone with respect.

This shall be the law of the leprous person for the day of his cleansing. He shall be brought to the priest (Leviticus 14:2). So begins a detailed description of the rituals involved with purifying someone who has been afflicted with Biblical Leprosy.

The original Hebrew word used in the Bible for this leprosy is *"Zaraat"*, which is commonly translated as leprosy. As all modern individuals are aware, however, leprosy is a medical affliction which, since the invention of antibiotics, is fully treatable medically. In referring to *"Zaraat"*, the Bible discusses a purely spiritual cleansing, performed by the priest. It is clear, therefore, that the word leprosy is actually a mistranslation of the word *"Zaraat"* and that the disease referred to in the Bible, although similar in its physical manifestations to leprosy or some other skin disease, is actually a spiritual ailment requiring a purely spiritual cure.

Although the Bible does not mention in these chapters in Leviticus what the cause of such an affliction would be, we do have a hint of the cause in a later chapter.

"Miriam and Aaron spoke against Moses because of the Cushite he had married... And the anger of the Lord was kindled against them... behold, Miriam was leprous, like snow" (NUMBERS 12:1-10).

Miriam was stricken by God with this same skin disease, clearly as a punishment for having spoken ill of her brother Moses.

God does not treat gossip lightly. As men and women created in His image, we are commanded to love our neighbor as ourselves and to treat everyone with respect. This includes not maligning them, even in a light, gossipy way. Our sages have said that if one shames another person in public it is as if he has murdered him. The import of this statement is that a person's honor, reputation and dignity are often as important to him as his physical life. When you damage a person's reputation, you are destroying an important part of his humanity. Similarly, when we gossip about people, we tarnish their reputation and cast a shadow upon their motivations or actions. When Miriam criticized Moses' relationship with his wife, she did just that and she was severely punished.

The issue of Zaraat is treated at length in the midrash and other commentaries of our sages. One of these commentaries lists seven different sins which result in Zaraat. The first one is gossip and slander, as explained above. The other six are: murder, false witness, sexual depravity, a course spirit, theft and envy. These are all sins that involve offense or damage to one's fellow human being. They all represent sins that affect societal norms and the impurity which forces the inflicted person to leave his community until he is purified represents a societal ban against him because of his anti-social behavior.

One of the most unusual aspects of the Zaraat infliction is when it affects a home rather than a person. Scripture tells us: ***"When you enter the Land of Canaan that I give you as a possession and I inflict an eruptive plagues upon a house in the land you***

possess" (LEVITICUS 14:34). In addition to the curious aspect of a house affliction, the language in this section is unique. The infliction on the house takes place only in the Land of Israel and it is a direct infliction by God. The verse reads ***"I inflict"*** in contrast to previous wordings ***"a person has on the skin of his body."*** The infliction here is so much more personal and so much more direct.

The midrash brings a fascinating interpretation to these verses. It notes that in most cases when Scripture introduces a subject regarding entering the land, it is a festive declaration coming to inspire or encourage. In this case, however, the infliction of Zaraat is hardly inspiring or encouraging.

The midrash explains: ***"When the Emorites heard that the Israelites are about to enter the land, they hid their valuables in the walls of their houses. God said to His people: I promised your forefathers that I would bring their children to a land of plenty. What did God do? He struck the house with afflictions, the Israelite owner took apart the house and found the treasure."***

This midrash turns the punishment of house afflictions into a reward for the Israelites who are entering the Land of Israel for the first time. And it reflects the spiritual reality that accompanies the entrance of the people to the Land. God promises Abraham that his children will inherit the land only after the sin of the Emorite comes due (GENESIS 15:16). And this midrash, in its typically concise but figurative way, shows how God is personally involved in judging the actions of the Emorites and through the affliction to their houses, representing their punishment, brings reward and bounty to the Nation of Israel.

We can influence our secular neighbors to embrace the Biblical values that have held our nation together for centuries.

Students studying Bible in the Study Hall of the Sussya High School

Acharei – Mot

Leviticus 16:1 – 18:30

We can influence our secular neighbors to embrace the Biblical values that have held our nation together for centuries.

Chapter 18 of Leviticus is seemingly a list of dos and don'ts, not unlike many of the rules of purity and impurity listed throughout Leviticus. But at closer examination, there is something different about the instructions listed here. The chapter begins with the verse:

"You shall not do as they do in the land of Egypt, where you lived, and you shall not do as they do in the land of Canaan, to which I am bringing you. You shall not walk in their statutes." (Leviticus 18:3)

Following this introductory verse is a list of incestual relationships that are forbidden. Included as well, however, are the prohibition against homosexuality and the prohibition against human sacrifice to the Molech.

Clearly, what connects all of these prohibitions is the fact that they were common in Egypt or in Canaan, or both. God's instruction, therefore, is not just about what is proper and improper behavior. It is an instruction against evil influences. It is these deeds that they have encountered in Egypt and will encounter in Canaan. In those countries, they are considered legitimate, but God brands them as abominations (Leviticus 18:29-30) and considers them to be a source of impurity for the nation (Leviticus 18:30).

There is a dynamic going on here that the Children of Israel were probably not even aware of at the time. They have just been selected out of the bonds of slavery in Egypt; they are living a supernatural existence in the desert; and they are preparing to enter the Promised Land. They may not yet realize that they are entering a land that is full of other nations, whose ways are unlike theirs and forbidden to the Children of Israel. God is warning them, in advance, not to be influenced by them – to shun the ways of the local peoples once they enter the Land.

The chapter ends with an incredible, spiritual statement that takes the previous admonition far beyond the issue of negative societal influences.

"For the people of the land, who were before you, did all of these abominations, so that the land became unclean, lest the land vomit you out when you make it unclean, as it vomited out the nation that was before you..." (LEVITICUS 18:27-28).

The land itself is affected by the abominations. It is unable to tolerate the presence of nations who so defile themselves and the land, that there is a physical reaction of the land itself – it vomits up those who have defiled it. God admonishes the Jewish people not to do the same as those nations before it. For if the Jewish people engage in the same sort of abominations, they too will be vomited out of the land.

In fact, we know from Jewish history, that the Jewish people were vomited out of the land. Particularly the first exile, the destruction of the First Temple, is recorded in the prophets as a punishment for abominations that defiled the land and forced the exile upon them.

"And I brought you into a plentiful land to enjoy its fruits and its good things. But when you came in, you defiled my land and made my heritage an abomination." (Jeremiah 2:7)

There is something very special, very supernatural about the Land of Israel, for it cannot tolerate the defilement.

Today, those of us who live in the Land of Israel and who read the Bible and take these verses seriously, are horrified at the growing level of ***"abominations"*** that exist in our holy land. Sexual impropriety and homosexuality are present in the land. Our Arab neighbors thrive on a modern form of worshipping the Molech – as they send their sons to be suicide bombers. The Bible is clear that all those who engage in these forbidden activities will be punished (Leviticus 18:29) but once the number of abominations reach a critical level, the people themselves will be vomited out.

The Jewish people are divided between secular and religious, and family values are not embraced by everyone. Will the balance shift in the negative direction? I hope and pray not. I hope that we can influence our secular neighbors to embrace the Biblical values that have held our nation together for centuries. God has promised us that He will return us to our land even after we have been thrown out. He has promised to help us return to Him and follow His ways (Deuteronomy 30). I believe that we are here to stay and that He will not throw us out again. But it is incumbent upon us to do whatever we can to ensure that the land is kept pure – that the abominations are eradicated.

Through acts of compassion and charity we can indeed become holy and worthy of the description, 'A kingdom of priests and a holy nation'.

Food packages for the needy in Efrat

Kedoshim

Leviticus 19:1 – 20:27

Through acts of compassion and charity we can indeed become holy and worthy of the description, ' A kingdom of priests and a holy nation'.

"*You shall be holy for I the Lord your God am holy*" (Leviticus 19:2). Throughout Leviticus, God commands Moses to teach the Children of Israel, or to instruct them in various commandments and rules of behavior. With this scripture, God introduces a few laws pertaining to our relationship with God, such as the Shabbat and the prohibition against idol worship. However, most of the commandments in this section relate to relationships within society, the treatment of the poor, honest employment practices and the very basic commandment to love one's neighbor as oneself.

But in the first commandment, which serves to introduce the entire chapter, God commands us to be holy. And to be holy because He is holy. In this brief instruction, we come to understand the very essence of man's relationship to God. God is perfection. God is holiness. And it is God that we must emulate. We must be holy because He is holy!

And how is that holiness expressed? Not like in so many other religions, exclusively through rituals and ceremonies. Yes, we do need to keep the Shabbat and bring the ritual sacrifices to God and not to pagan idols. But that is dealt with so briefly. The thrust of the chapter is the expectation of holiness in our dealings with our fellow man.

"You shall not oppress your neighbor or rob him, the wages of a hired servant shall not remain with you all night until the morning. You shall not curse the deaf or put a stumbling block before the blind, but you shall fear your God: I am the Lord." (LEVITICUS 19:13-14)

These two verses present just one example of the density of the laws mentioned in this portion, their universal morality and their connection with God. The original Hebrew word for ***"shall not remain with you all night"*** is ***"talin"***, a word that literally means to stay overnight. In modern Hebrew, this word is used to describe the act of delaying a salary payment, which is illegal under Israeli law. It is this very verse that has served as the basis for the modern Israeli statute.

The prohibition against putting a stumbling block before the blind has been interpreted to include any action that would tempt someone to commit a sin who is without the knowledge or inner resources to resist the temptation. Just as a blind person is unable to see the physical obstacle before him and will therefore stumble, so too, a person with a known weakness for kleptomania, for example, should not be left alone in a shop, for he will be unable to comprehend the moral obstacle to theft and will help himself to the shop's goods. This becomes society's responsibility, not just the responsibility of the potential thief.

Interestingly, this prohibition against placing obstacles in a blind man's way has also been used by the rabbis to teach us the importance of taking responsibility for the spiritual welfare of an individual. A religious Jew is well versed in God's word. He keeps the Sabbath and honors God's other commandments. He must be very careful, therefore, not to invite a transgression from his fellow

Jew who might not be aware of the commandments. For example, if he is visiting a secular friend on Shabbat, he should be careful not to complain that he is hungry so as not to inadvertently suggest that his friend cook for him on Shabbat, a violation of God's holy day. While this may seem very technical, it is actually an expression of the incredibly profound level of caring that we have, not only for our fellow man's physical welfare but for his spiritual welfare as well.

These verses, like so many others, end with the words ***"I am the Lord."*** The moral imperatives listed in this portion are all intimately connected with our relationship with God. The portion begins with the statement that we must be holy for God is holy. The continuation of the chapter represents the fullness of this concept of emulating God's ways: God is compassionate, and we must emulate this characteristic of God as well. For it is through our relationships with our fellow human beings, through acts of compassion and charity that we can indeed become holy and, as a people, become worthy of the description that God himself assigns to the people of Israel: ***"A kingdom of priests and a holy nation"*** (Exodus 19:6).

Judaism is not just a religion – it is a nationality.

The Israeli flag at the Western Wall, adjacent to the Temple Mount

Emor

Leviticus 21:1 – 24:23

The child of a mixed marriage between a Jew and a non-Jew will always be confused, will lack a clear identity and will have trouble relating to God.

This week's portion includes laws regarding the holidays as well as restrictions and instructions to the priests. The final section of the portion, however, begins with a rather unusual story:

"Now an Israelite woman's son, whose father was an Egyptian, went out among the people of Israel. And the Israelite woman's son and a man of Israel fought in the camp, and the Israelite woman's son blasphemed the Name, and cursed. Then they brought him to Moses. His mother's name was Shelomith, the daughter of Dibri, of the tribe of Dan." (Leviticus 24:10-11)

The people then awaited God's judgment of this man and it was swift indeed. God commands Moses to have this man stoned and then instructs Moses that the penalty for cursing God is death.

Following this story and the accompanying instruction is a series of punishments for various injuries. What I found particularly unusual in this section, however, is that the listing of laws for the various personal injuries, for murder and for cursing God, is embedded in an actual incident. And when the instructions are completed, Scripture concludes with the actual implementation of the punishment, the stoning, in the particular incident described.

The story itself is told in an unusual way. We don't know the name of the man who has cursed God but we know that his mother is an Israelite while his father is Egyptian. What is the relevance of this description? We are also told the name of his mother and her tribal affiliation. Why is this relevant?

The Midrash and later commentaries noted these difficulties. Rashi, the classic 11th century commentator draws from Midrashic sources to explain the entire situation. The man in question is the child of a mixed marriage – an Israelite mother and an Egyptian father. His mother's name is listed in order to clarify her status – she has a family and is a member of the tribe of Dan. However, the tribal affiliation of a man is based on his father's tribe and since this man's father is an Egyptian, he is left without a tribal identity.

The Midrash fills in the details, based on these facts as mentioned in Scripture, as follows: The man in question wants to pitch his tent with the tribe of Dan but they don't accept him since he is not of their tribe. He argues with a man of the tribe and they approach Moses for judgment. Moses decides against him – he is a man with no tribal status, as his father is not an Israelite. The man is furious and curses God. The result is fatal.

The personal status of the curser as described in the Scripture and as explained further by the Midrash is a difficult one indeed. The Midrash further points out that he has chosen to affiliate with the Jewish people, as noted by the words ***"among the people of Israel"*** (LEVITICUS 24:10). But he cannot invent a tribe for himself. Without an Israelite father, that tribal status is missing. For the generation which left Egypt and the next generation which will enter the Land of Israel, this status is critical for it determines the right to territory in the Land of Israel.

Of course none of this justifies cursing God, but it does present a profound understanding of the need for national identity and the difficulties which arise when there is a mixed marriage. National identity matters. And in Biblical times, tribal identity mattered. A man whose heritage is mixed is a troubled and frustrated man. It is no coincidence that it is this man who has cursed God. For he has not found himself in God. He is not sure of who he is and, therefore, he is unable to accept his place among God's people.

Perhaps if the man in question had truly felt a part of the Jewish people and accepted his identity as an Israelite, he would not have cursed God but would have asked Moses to help him find an appropriate solution. But in cursing God, he also proved that he hadn't fully shed his Egyptian identity.

In the modern world, when nationality is a much more fluid concept than it used to be, and people immigrate from country to country, mixed marriage is a rarely used term. But in Judaism, it is still critical. Judaism is not just a religion – it is a nationality. And it is a faith community. The child of a mixed marriage between a Jew and a non-Jew will always be confused, will lack a clear identity and will have trouble relating to God for he will not be coming to God as a member of one community.

For six years you shall sow your field, and for six years you shall prune your vineyard and gather in its fruits.

A private garden in Karnei Shomron, Samaria

Behar

Leviticus 25:1 – 26:2

The Sabbath reminds us that God created the world and we are commanded to rest one day each week, to stop our activities of work and creation and devote ourselves to God.

This week's portion opens with the laws of the Sabbatical year and the Jubilee. The first section describes the Sabbatical year:

"When you come into the land that I give you, the land shall observe a Sabbatical year for the Lord. For six years you may sow your field and for six years you may prune your vineyard; and you may gather up its crop." (Leviticus 25:3-4)

The words used in this section are all related to the Sabbath or ***"Shabbat"*** as it is known in Hebrew, and parallel the words found in the Ten Commandments regarding the observance of the Sabbath.

In the Ten Commandments we read: ***"Six days you shall labor, and do all your work. But the seventh day is a Sabbath to the Lord your God. On it you shall not do any work, you, or your son, or your daughter, your male servant, or your female servant, or your livestock, or the sojourner who is within your gate."*** (Exodus 20:9-10)

In this week's portion, we read: ***"For six years you shall sow your field, and for six years you shall prune your vineyard and gather in its fruits. But in the seventh year there shall be a Sabbath***

of solemn rest for the land, a Sabbath to the Lord. You shall not sow your field or prune your vineyard. You shall not reap what grows of itself in your harvest, or gather the grapes of your undressed vine. It shall be a year of solemn rest for the land." (LEVITICUS 25:3-5)

The English translation, however, does not do justice to the extent to which the concept of Sabbath, through the recurring use of the Hebrew word Shabbat, is stressed in this passage. The Hebrew is as follows: ***"But in the seventh year there shall be a Shabbat Shabatton for the land, a Shabbat to the Lord... It shall be a year of Shabbaton for the land."*** The Hebrew Shabbaton, a derivative of the Hebrew word Shabbat, is used to denote solemn rest.

This passage, therefore, is all about the Sabbath. But rather than discuss the Sabbath that we observe each week, as we rest on the seventh day, this Sabbath refers to the land, the year of rest that must be observed in the seventh year.

The Jubilee is a further Sabbath. After seven Sabbatical years, there is a fiftieth year of Jubilee. In addition to the celebration, the blowing of the trumpets, there is a profound message of freedom and restitution implicit in the Jubilee. The verse inscribed on the famous Liberty Bell in Philadelphia, symbol of the freedom the US has always prided itself on, is found in this section:

"And you shall consecrate the fiftieth year, and proclaim liberty throughout the land to all its inhabitants. It shall be a jubilee for you, when each of you shall return to his property and each of you shall return to his clan." (LEVITICUS 25:10).

Loans taken in previous years are forgiven, land transferred in previous years is returned to its rightful owners, keeping the tribal territories inviolate. This is truly a declaration of freedom, for any man who sold his land or any man sold into slavery to relieve a debt, is now free again. This freedom is endowed upon us by God!

"The land shall not be sold in perpetuity, for the land is mine. For you are strangers and sojourners with me." (LEVITICUS 25:23)

Providing further understanding of the reversion of the land to its original owner, this verse extends beyond the context of real property transactions. This verse tells us, in no uncertain terms, that the Land of Israel belongs to God. Our presence in the land must be in line with His guidelines and His restrictions. And those restrictions include a verse in Deuteronomy:

"and when the Lord your God gives them over to you, and you defeat them, then you must devote them to complete destruction. You shall make no covenant with them and show no mercy to them" (DEUTERONOMY 7:2)

The words ***"show no mercy to them"*** are a translation of the Hebrew ***"Lo Techanem."*** An alternative translation of those words, found in the Talmud is: ***"do not give them a place,"*** or do not enable the nations to have a place in the land. This is consistent with the verse in our portion – the land belongs to God and only He has the right to determine who can take possession of it.

The Sabbath reminds us that God created the world and we are commanded to rest one day each week, to stop our activities of work and creation and devote ourselves to spiritual pursuits. The land does the same in the seventh year and reverts to its original owner in the 50th year, after seven Sabbatical cycles. The message is the same – the land belongs to God and only He can determine who may possess it, who may cultivate it and when.

With the return to the biblical areas of Jerusalem, Judea and Samaria, God's name is being sanctified each day.

Ethiopian immigrants study at the Lehava High School in Kedumim

BEHUKOTAI

LEVITICUS 26:3 – 27:34

With the stunning victory in 1967 and the return to the biblical areas of Jerusalem, Judea and Samaria, God's name is being sanctified each day.

"If you walk in my statutes and observe my commandments and do them, then I will give you your rains in their season, and the land shall yield its increase... I will give peace in the land." (LEVITICUS 26:3-6)

So begins a critical chapter in the Bible, one that sets forth clearly God's expectations from His people and the rewards and punishments that follow obedience or disobedience respectively. Amazingly, all of the rewards and punishments are connected with the Land of Israel. If we follow God's word, He will reward us with peace and prosperity in our land. If we disobey Him, we will be exiled and spread among enemy nations.

But God concludes this chapter with a fabulous statement, a promise that the Jewish people took with them into exile, time and time again.

"Yet for all that, when they are in the land of their enemies, I will not spurn them, neither will I abhor them so as to destroy them utterly and break my covenant with them, for I am the Lord their God." (LEVITICUS 26:44)

For centuries, anti-Semitism was fueled by a belief that God had abandoned His people, that the promises that had been listed specifically in the Bible for the Jewish people were no longer relevant. Medieval Christian theologies were based on this premise. But it is the clear statement in verse 44 that belies this idea, for God explicitly states that despite exile and deserved punishment, God will never break His covenant with us.

Interestingly, God anticipated this phenomenon and addressed it through His prophets:

"But when they came to the nations, wherever they came, they profaned my holy name, in that people said of them, 'These are the people of the Lord, and yet they had to go out of his land.' But I had concern for my holy name, which the house of Israel had profaned among the nations to which they came. Therefore say to the house of Israel, Thus says the Lord God, It is not for your sake, O house of Israel, that I am about to act, but for the sake of my holy name ... And the nations will know that I am the Lord, declares the Lord God, when through you I vindicate my holiness before their eyes." (EZEKIEL 36:20-23)

The people of Israel have sinned and they have been exiled as their punishment. But the very exile of the People of God causes a desecration of His name, for the nations remark, disparagingly, if these are the people of the Lord, then why have they been removed from their land? The apparent abandonment by God of His people causes the nations to doubt the very promise, to question the veracity of God's word – a profound desecration of His name. Therefore, God assures us that He will return us to our land, if only to vindicate this desecration. And in vindicating this desecration, the nations will understand that God, indeed, has never broken His covenant with us.

The Holocaust was the greatest desecration of God's name in history. Six million Jews, God's people, were murdered in gas chambers, starved in ghettos and shot before mass graves. So many of these Jews cried out to God and declared ***"Hear O Israel the Lord is our God the Lord is one"*** just before their death, trying to sanctify His name as they were martyred for their Judaism. But the darkness and evil that permeated Europe, brought the question to so many lips, both Jewish and non Jewish – Where was God? Can there be a greater desecration of His name?

Israel was the response to this question. The establishment of the State and the ingathering of the exiles was the greatest miracle of all time.

With the establishment of the State of Israel and, later on, with the stunning victory in 1967 and the return to the biblical areas of Jerusalem, Judea and Samaria, many in the nations began to reject the doctrines that formed the basis of anti-Semitism and realized that God had not abandoned His people. Indeed, with the return of the Jewish people to the Land of Israel, God's name is being sanctified, daily.

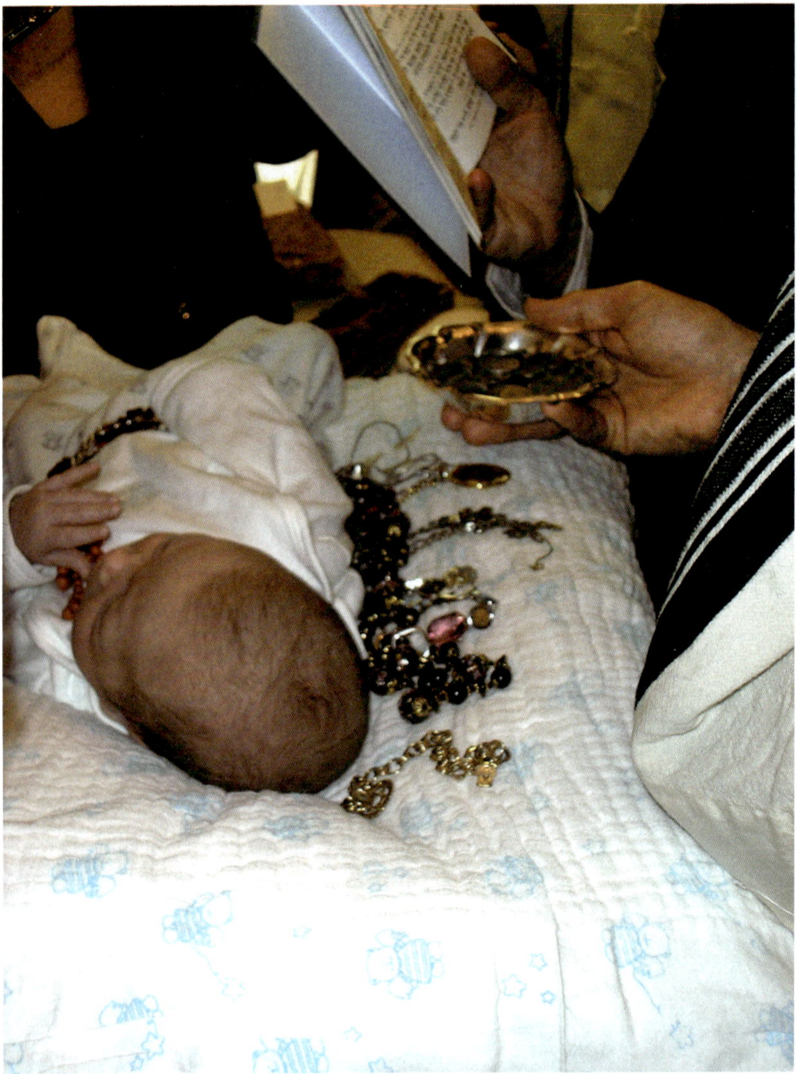

The first-born are especially dear to God.

A one-month old baby boy is "redeemed" by a priest in modern Israel *(Photo: Avi Dror)*

Bamidbar

Numbers 1:1 – 4:20

To this day, all first-born sons to a Jewish mother are 'redeemed' in a special ceremony which represents the divine statement that the Nation of Israel is holy.

The Hebrew word for the Book of Numbers is ***"Bamidbar"***, which means 'desert' for it narrates the events that occurred while the people of Israel were wandering in the wilderness. In fact, it is in this book of the Bible that we learn of the sin of the spies which results in the Children of Israel spending 40 long years in the desert.

But the name ***"Numbers"*** is actually very appropriate as a name of this book, and especially of this week's portion, since the portion is mostly concerned with the census of the Children of Israel. Our sages say that God's counting of His children is a sign of His love for us, similar to the way a person will count his treasures and make sure they are all where they need to be.

I would like to focus on one small aspect of the census. There is a separate census of the Levites and of the first-born of all of Israel, and God designates the Levites as His special servants, in place of the first-born.

"Behold, I have taken the Levites from among the people of Israel instead of every firstborn who opens the womb among the people of Israel. The Levites shall be mine, for all the firstborn

are mine. On the day that I struck down all the firstborn in the land of Egypt, I consecrated for my own all the firstborn in Israel, both of man and of beast. They shall be mine: I am the Lord." (NUMBERS 3:12-13)

These two verses contain such a powerful message. When God sent the angel of death to kill all the first-born of Egypt, the Children of Israel were instructed to put blood on the door posts of their homes, so the angel of death would skip over them. And, indeed, every first-born in Egypt was killed, except the first-born of Israel. And from that day forward, says God, the first born of Israel are special to him. For when He saved them, He set them aside as holy to Him.

It seems that the first-born would, therefore, have been those chosen to serve God in the Tabernacle and later in the Temple, but then God instructs the Levites to take their place. And, in fact, when the final census is taken, the difference in numbers between the Levites and the first-born must be redeemed in a special ceremony (NUMBERS 3:45-51). But nowhere in the Bible does it say why this change took place.

Rashi, a famous 11th century Jewish commentator, noted an ancient Jewish tradition that this switch came as a result of the sinning of the Children of Israel with the Golden Calf. The only people who did not join the worshipping frenzy were the tribe of the Levites and, in fact, it is the Levites who assist Moses in punishing the sinners. It is the children of Levi who respond to Moses' call ***"Who is on the Lord's side? Come to me"*** (EXODUS 32:26). Since the Levites did not sin against God with this horrible sin of idol worship, betraying God who had just redeemed them from Egypt and given them the Torah at Sinai, they and only they would be able to serve God on behalf of the entire people of Israel in the Temple.

To this day, all first-born sons to a Jewish mother are redeemed, at the age of one month, in a special ceremony in which the father of the child gives five silver pieces to a member of the priestly group of Levi, a Cohen. Until this redemption takes place, the first-born is dedicated to God. But, as a result of the sin of the Golden Calf, that first-born is not able to serve God in the Temple. He must be redeemed and exchanged with a Levite.

The modern redemption process essentially serves to remind us not only of the ancient ceremony that took place in the desert as noted in Numbers 3, but represents the divine statement that the Nation of Israel is holy. The first-born are especially dear to God, as He saved the first-born of Israel even as He destroyed the first-born of the Egyptians. The Levites are holy and special for their devotion to God, even as the rest of the nation sinned, and for their subsequent selection to serve God in the Tabernacle. And the entire nation is ***"a kingdom of priests and a holy nation"*** (Exodus 19:6).

The "Nazirite" takes an oath of abstention from wine, refrains from coming into contact with a dead body, and grows his hair wild.

Boutique winery in Psagot

Naso

Numbers 4:21 – 7:89

It is indeed a challenge to aspire to holiness while living in an incredibly secular world. But that is the lesson of the "Nazirite" and that is the ultimate challenge.

This week's portion includes the laws regarding the *"Nazirite"* who takes an oath of abstention from wine, refrains from coming into contact with a dead body, and grows his hair wild. The Nazirite is a sort of ascetic who seeks to withdraw from some of the material concerns of daily life in an attempt to become holier.

There are many religions around the world whose focus is on asceticism. In those religions, the ideal person of faith is one who abstains from contact with the material world, including business, sexual relations, and fancy food and drink. The Bible, however, sets forth a specific formula for the ascetic to follow. He abstains from only three things – wine, contact with a dead body and hair-grooming. His period of asceticism is restricted to a specific period of time which he chooses. The ascetic period does not interfere with family life and it does not last forever.

At the conclusion of the ascetic period, the Nazirite brings two sacrifices – a sin offering and a feast offering. This, in and of itself, reflects the complexity of the ascetic period. On the one hand, the Nazirite concludes a period of holiness and he is celebrating that extra closeness to God that he has attained by bringing the feast offering. However, the sin offering indicates that there is something missing during this period; that the actions of the Nazirite may include some element of sin.

Scripture does, indeed, reflect a complex attitude toward the Nazirite, and Jewish commentaries have long debated the positive or negative value of this ascetic option. But what is so special about this chapter is the fact that it exists at all. Judaism is replete with laws and customs, most of which have either been mandated directly by the Bible or have been connected with specific Biblical imperatives. Throughout Scripture, God refers to the Jewish nation as a holy nation and enjoins His people to be holy (EXODUS 19:6, LEVITICUS 19:2). And yet, there is no commandment anywhere to retreat from worldly activities. In fact, the Bible takes for granted and encourages marital relations, celebrations that include food and bountiful harvests. These are not the activities of the ascetic, in the standard sense of the word.

It is interesting to note that the requirement that a Nazirite abstain from wine reflects an understanding that wine is an acceptable part of ordinary life. While drunkenness is certainly not tolerated, moderate amounts of wine are taken for granted. In fact, every Jewish ceremony, from ancient times to today, includes a blessing over wine, whether it be the Shabbat and holiday meals, a wedding ceremony, or the circumcision of a baby boy.

When Scripture selects, however, a few earthly pleasures that will be foregone by the Nazirite, it selects those pleasures that are not considered essential to daily life. And wine, while permitted, is certainly not essential. Not so marital relations, for family is key in Jewish life.

Actually, the rules pertaining to the Nazirite reflect an incredible wisdom and understanding as to human nature.

Generally, people are expected to aspire to holiness while carrying out their daily lives. However, the Bible recognizes that, at times, some individuals may feel the need to separate themselves from the world for a brief period, to try and attain a level of holiness which they perceive as too difficult to attain through ordinary activities. In that case, an individual is allowed to swear a Nazirite oath – but it is limited. It is limited in time and the actual areas of abstention are limited. And unlike so many other religions, a Nazirite does not abstain from marital relationships!

It is indeed a challenge to aspire to holiness while living in an incredibly secular world. But that is the ultimate challenge. While the Nazirite may have attained a higher level of holiness and, therefore, brings a feast offering, he was not able to attain that same holy level while acting within societal norms. For that reason, he brings a sin offering. But how incredible it is that the Bible has allowed for all sorts of individuals to attain holiness in the ways that best suit them.

'Arise, O Lord, and let your enemies be scattered, and let those who hate you flee before you'.

Security is a necessity for the people of Alon

Behaalotcha

Numbers 8:1 – 12:16

God has always been leading us towards Redemption, and ever since the establishment of the State of Israel in 1948, we have eagerly awaited the completion of the process.

And whenever the ark set out, Moses said, ***"Arise, O Lord, and let your enemies be scattered, and let those who hate you flee before you."*** And when it rested, he said, ***"Return, O Lord, to the ten thousand thousands of Israel"*** (Numbers 10:35- 36).

In the Hebrew text, there is an inverted Hebrew letter ***"nun"*** placed before and after these two verses, a one-of-a-kind symbol in the Scriptures. Clearly, these two verses are meant to be set apart, to draw our attention to something dramatic.

And, in fact, these verses mark a highlight in the experience of the Children of Israel in the desert. Until this point, we have read of the counting of the Children of Israel, of the dedication of the Tabernacle and the procession of the camp, as each tribe gathers around its flag. Revelation at Sinai happened the year before, God has forgiven His people after the sin of the golden calf, the Tabernacle has been built and dedicated, the priests have been instructed in their duties and the camp is organized and ready to march. And in fact, these two verses signify their marching orders. We have already learned that the camp travels only when the holy cloud is lifted, and here, Moses calls upon God to rise up, to lift the cloud and the nation will march forward, into the Land of Israel.

The journey should only take 11 days. They have already traveled 3 days (NUMBERS 10:33). But with the opening verse of Chapter 11, everything begins to crash. The nation complains repeatedly and is punished. Miriam speaks ill of her brother and his wife and is punished. And then, of course, comes the sin of the spies, resulting in the most severe punishment of all – an entire generation would die in the desert and never see the Promised Land.

These two verses promise what could have been. These two verses echo the trumpets that were about to be sounded and the royal procession that would have brought the Nation of Israel into the Land of Israel within weeks. Instead, it would be 38 more years.

And 38 years later, we encounter a similar phrase: ***"When the people set out from their encampment to cross the Jordan, the priests bearing the Ark of the Covenant were at the head of the people"*** (JOSHUA 3:14). Whereas in Numbers, it is the ark which sets out, in Joshua, it is the people who set out, with the ark mentioned afterwards as leading the way.

I believe that the verse in Joshua is intentionally reminding us of the previous verse but the similarity is for purposes of contrast. In Numbers, the ark was ready to travel but the people weren't, lacking the faith that would be needed to trust God and embark on such an adventure. In Joshua, the next generation is ready for their grand entry into the Land – it is the people who set out, following the direction of the Ark.

The State of Israel was established in 1948 among much fanfare and trumpet-blowing, both the trumpets of war (unfortunately) and the trumpets of God's miracles. Ever since, we have eagerly awaited the completion of the process, the final resting in the Land of Israel, in peace with our neighbors. But so many things went wrong. So many of our people did not really understand the spiritual significance of these events. We are ready to march forward, but God may be putting a hold on the procession for now. Will we have to wait a generation until we proceed? We don't know. But we must continue reading these verses, calling upon God to rise and lead us into the Promised Land, for even if there is a delay, He will surely lead us on to redemption.

Moses sends the leaders of the twelve tribes of Israel to check out the Land of Israel... to taste the fruits and crops and determine the fertility of the land.

A Malyasian Christian and an Israeli child plant a fruit tree in Karnei Shomron

Shelach

Numbers 13:1 – 15:41

God has prepared His people to receive the ultimate gift – a land that He created especially for them, and just as they are about to receive the gift, they reject it.

Moses sends the leaders of the twelve tribes of Israel to check out the Land of Israel, to investigate its people and evaluate their strength or weakness, to taste the fruits and crops and determine the fertility of the land. The expectation is high and, indeed, the spies return with a report that the land flows with milk and honey. They bring back the fruit of the land to demonstrate its juiciness and sweetness.

But they also bring back a bitter report, that the land is full of giants and fortified cities. Despite the obvious natural riches that the spies observed, they reach a horrifying conclusion: ***"We are not able to go up against the people, for they are stronger than we are. So they brought to the people of Israel a bad report of the land..."*** (Numbers 13:31 32).

Clearly, the spies were lacking in faith. They observed the fortifications, but didn't take into account the fact that God would protect them and would ensure their victory.

Interestingly, though, it is not their lack of faith that Scripture refers to in summarizing the punishment brought upon these spies. It is the fact that they have slandered the land, bringing evil words before the people of Israel.

"And the men whom Moses sent to spy out the land, who returned and made all the congregation grumble against him by bringing up a bad report about the land; the men who brought up a bad report of the land died by plague before the Lord." (NUMBERS 14:36-37)

The Land of Israel is not just a gift that God has given to His people. It is a land that He set aside for them from the beginning of mankind. ***"Remember the days of old, Consider the years of ages past; Ask your father, he will inform you, Your elders, they will tell you. When the Most High gave nations their homes And set the divisions of Man, He fixed the boundaries of people In relation to the number of the Children of Israel"*** (DEUTERONOMY 32:7-8). God did not just give us the Land. He divided up the lands of the rest of the nations only after he had first set aside the Land of Israel for His people.

God has prepared His people to receive the ultimate gift – a land that He created especially for them, that He designated for them from Creation and revealed His purpose to their forefather Abraham. And just as they are about to receive the gift, they reject it. Yes, they are afraid of the enemies that await them in the land, but they go beyond an expression of fear. They turn away God's precious gift.

In 1948 and again in 1967, God presented this gift to His people once more. The State of Israel was created and later, the Biblical Heartland was liberated. This was the result of military victory, but the miracle of it all embodied God's gift to His people. But instead of accepting the gift and trusting in Him to assist us in holding on to it, there were people within Israel who rejected the gift outright. Out of fear, indeed, but they rejected it nonetheless. And as the years progressed, these same people began to slander the land, calling it a land, ***"that devours its inhabitants"*** (Numbers 13:32), a land which will know no peace unless the people of Israel abandon it.

Yes, the land has been slandered and God surely trembles at the sound of such terrible words. There are a dedicated few who defend the land at every juncture, who cling to it with every fiber of their being. But will this be enough to protect us all?

God sets the stage for a nation who will be able to obey God, with the help of its leaders.

Rabbi Natan Greenberg, Dean of the Bat Ayin Yeshiva, has a spiritual vision of religious Zionism

Korach

Numbers 16:1 – 18:32

The Torah is premised upon acceptance of authority and the key to the continuity of the nation is the requirement to accept righteous leadership and to listen to their instruction.

This week's portion tells the story of the rebellion of Korach. The portion begins with two verses that set forth exactly who is part of the rebellious group:

"Now Korach the son of Izhar, son of Kohath, son of Levi, and Dathan and Abiram the sons of Eliab, and On the son of Peleth, sons of Reuben, took men. And they rose up before Moses, with a number of the people of Israel, 250 chiefs of the congregation, chosen from the assembly, well-known men." (Numbers16:1-2)

The rebels consisted of Korach and his group of Levites, Dathan and Abiram and On, from the tribe of Reuben, and 250 representatives of the rest of the tribes.

Throughout the conversations with Moses, the actual charges of the rebels reflect their differing backgrounds. Korach's main complaint, which is essentially a Levite complaint, is that the entire nation is holy, so why are Moses and Aaron raising themselves above the rest. Moses' response to this claim is directed at the Levites – is it not enough that the Levites have been given special positions in the service of God, that they also demand the priesthood, that very special position reserved only for the children of Aaron? (Numbers 16: 8-11).

The next claim is voiced by Dathan and Abiram. They accuse Moses of taking them out of Egypt and, rather than bringing them to a wonderful land, they are brought to the desert. In an ironic twist of the Biblical vision, Dathan and Abiram refer to Egypt as a land of milk and honey, and refute Moses' claim that the Children of Israel will enter a land of milk and honey. Furthermore, Dathan and Abiram attack the leadership of Moses and Aaron by refusing to come when he calls them (NUMBERS 16:12-14). Moses' response to this addresses the leadership challenge only, not the accusation regarding the Exodus itself: ***"I have not taken even one ass from them!"*** (NUMBERS 16:15)

Moses has been so honorable in his dealings with the people, totally lacking in self-interest, devoting himself only to the good of the people. He seems personally hurt by this attack.

But the attack on the very Exodus from Egypt remains unanswered. This claim is actually reminiscent of the complaints lodged by the Children of Israel just after the spies returned with their evil report from their reconnaissance mission in the Land of Israel (NUMBERS 14:2-3). In fact, at the conclusion of that incident, God punishes the entire generation, declaring that they would all die in the desert, that only their children would enter the Land. So when Dathan and Abiram complain that Moses has taken them from Egypt only to die in the desert, they speak a certain truth. They just leave out the fact that this was the result of sin, not of original design.

The 250 men don't make a specific claim of their own but they are dealt with separately – they are commanded to bring an incense offering and are killed in the process. These individuals are leaders of the various tribes, as they are referred to as ***"well-known men"*** and their claim is also a challenge to the hegemony of Moses and Aaron's leadership. In response, they are given the opportunity to perform a priestly task, the incense offering, and God Himself reveals the fraud of their claim to leadership, as they are killed by a fire from heaven. All of this points to the fact that the claims raised by the rebels were not substantive in nature. They were excuses. The key to the rebellion is the rejection of the authority of Moses and Aaron, which ultimately entails the rejection of the authority of God. For it is God who appointed Moses and Aaron as leaders. And, perhaps, for that reason, the death of Korach's faction was so supernatural – the ground opened up and swallowed them alive!

The entire Torah is premised upon acceptance of authority – God's authority and the authority of those whom He has appointed as our leaders.

"And you shall come to the Levitical priests and to the judge who is in office in those days, and you shall consult them, and they shall declare to you the decision. Then you shall do according to what they declare to you from that place that the Lord will choose. And you shall be careful to do according to all that they direct you. According to the instructions that they give you, and according to the decision which they pronounce to you, you shall do." (Deuteronomy 17:9-10)

God took the Children of Israel out of Egypt and established them as a nation, providing them with their first leaders, men of righteousness and generosity. But key to the continuity of the nation as God's people, in obedience to His word, is the requirement to accept the righteous leadership and to listen to their instruction.

In responding to Korach's rebellion as swiftly and decisively as Moses does, and as God does, God sets the stage for a nation who will be able to obey God, with the help of its leaders. But Moses' statement in response to Dothan and Abiram's challenge establishes a guideline for all future leaders – they must be devoted to the people, without self-interest or dishonesty of any kind.

"Shall we bring water for you out of this rock?"

Fellowship Church in Florida help build the waterfall park in Kedumim

Hukat

Numbers 19:1 – 22:1

The victories that Israel has experienced in the many wars against her were miracles, direct gifts from God, which we must recognize and acknowledge.

Numbers 20 presents a fascinating story, the story of the death of Miriam and the subsequent loss of water.

"And the people stayed in Kadesh. And Miriam died there and was buried there. Now there was no water for the congregation." (Numbers 20:1-2)

Clearly, Miriam's life is associated with water; upon her death there is a sudden lack of water. This association with water is actually seen earlier, just after the parting of the Red Sea. Miriam sings her song of praise to God as she stands on the banks of the Red Sea, which has drowned the Egyptian enemies. She is surrounded by water, albeit sea water. Immediately thereafter, the nation complains of a lack of drinking water (Exodus 15:22-25). God then provides the water needed for drinking which remains plentiful until Miriam's death.

Then begins the story of Moses and Aaron bringing forth water from the rock, that has had centuries of Bible scholars puzzled. What exactly did Moses and Aaron do wrong to have warranted God's terrible wrath and punishment:

"Because you did not believe in me, to uphold me as holy in the eyes of the people of Israel, therefore you shall not bring this assembly into the land that I have given them." (Numbers 20:12)

Some commentators have noted the difference between God's commandment to Moses and Aaron to speak to the rock and Moses and Aaron's actual action, which included hitting the rock. Because Moses and Aaron had assembled the entire Nation of Israel and were about to demonstrate a tremendous miracle of God, bringing water from a dry rock, it was vital that they obey the letter of God's instruction, so as to ensure the miracle exactly as God had intended.

I have always been troubled by this interpretation. After all, going to Israel is what Moses and Aaron had dreamed of and remained loyal to more than anyone else in the nation. To deprive them of this dream for such a technical error seems difficult to understand.

I would like to suggest a slightly different interpretation. Yes, the fact that Moses and Aaron had gathered the entire nation to witness the miracle is critical. It is moments like these that can make all the difference – the difference between a tremendous sanctification of God's name and the absence of such sanctification. Pay attention, though, to what Moses actually says to the nation: ***"Shall we bring water for you out of this rock?"*** They don't say – watch how God will draw water from this rock, but rather, ***"we"*** will draw water. They missed the point – and they missed a tremendous opportunity to sanctify God's name. They hit the rock and made it look as if there were some magical powers in the staff that made the rock bring forth the water. When actually, this was God's doing.

There is no question in my mind that Moses and Aaron were well aware that it was God's miracle that they were taking part in. But they missed the opportunity to demonstrate that in no uncertain terms to the Children of Israel. And that is the meaning of God's statement to them: ***"You did not believe in me, to uphold me as holy in the eyes of the people of Israel."***

This is a powerful lesson, indeed. For it behooves us all, as human beings, to recognize God's hand in daily events in our lives and in the lives of nations. And we must declare that hand of God, not just understand it within our own selves. I believe that the victories that Israel has experienced in the many wars against her, especially during Israel's War of Independence, when Israel survived as a new state, and the Six Day War, when Israel regained control of the heart of Biblical Israel, were miracles, direct gifts from God. Perhaps if more of us were to declare that in public, in recognition of what God has given us, He would enable us not only to enter the land, but to dwell there in peace and security.

Our traditions and our faith are different from others.

A young woman prays at Biblical Shiloh *(Photo: Ancient Shiloh)*

Balak

Numbers 22:1 – 25:9

Our traditions and faith are different from others. Balaam taught us that if we stay true to those values that we inherited from our forefathers, we will always be blessed.

The story of Balaam and his desire to curse the Children of Israel is a fabulous one. At the request of Balak, King of Moab, Balaam tries to curse Israel, but at each opportunity, God prevents him from doing so. Finally, left with no other choice, he blesses the Nation of Israel in some of the most beautiful verses in the Bible.

"And Balaam lifted up his eyes and saw Israel camping tribe by tribe. And the Spirit of God came upon him... How lovely are your tents, O Jacob, your encampments, O Israel." (Numbers 24:2-5)

The Book of Numbers begins with the national census and the Children of Israel are counted based on their families, the ***"houses of their fathers."*** This reflects an important development in the nation, for as the families of the Children of Israel become the Nation of Israel, the significant unit of identity is the family.

And indeed, it is this family unity, this dwelling according to their tribes and within their tents that attracts Balaam. Our sages noted that what Balaam actually saw within the camp of Israel was an incredible sense of modesty and respect for each other's privacy. The openings of the tents were set up in such a way that they did not face the openings of the neighboring tents, allowing each family some minimum degree of privacy. And each tent belonged to a family, for there is holiness in the family unit.

It could not have been easy for millions of people to live in such close quarters and in temporary dwellings for so many years. Although there are numerous accounts in the book of Numbers of the people questioning God or of their lack of appreciation for the miracle of their lives, there isn't a single account of family disputes or neighborly quarrels. And while we can assume that there was a certain amount of this, it clearly was not significant, or it would have been mentioned. Instead, we have Balaam's account of the goodness of the tents of Israel.

As an outsider, Balaam was attracted to this idea of family harmony, within the context of national unity. This was an idea that was foreign to the Canaanite nations of the time, a culture that was permeated with pagan values and child sacrifice.

Interestingly, there is no indication that the Children of Israel knew of Balaam's attempt to curse Israel and his subsequent blessing of them, for there is no interaction between Balaam and the Children of Israel at any part of the story. Balaam stands upon the mountains of Moab and views the new nation from afar without their awareness. And what he sees is a blessing.

Throughout the centuries, the Jewish family has been the basis of the continued existence of our nation. Father and Mother took upon themselves to teach their children the heritage of our forefathers and the teachings of the Bible. Family meals have also been a key element in the celebration of the Biblical holidays. Marriage and children are key values in Judaism, way beyond the personal enjoyment that progeny can bring. And it is the family unit that has enabled us to preserve our heritage and our uniqueness.

The Jews are frequently concerned with how they are viewed by the world. Our traditions and our faith, however, are different from others and we tend to fear the worst among those who view us from afar. But Balaam taught us an important lesson – if we stay true to those values we inherited from our forefathers, we will always be blessed. Even those who would curse us will have no choice but to bless us.

And Balaam echoes God's promise to Abraham: ***"Blessed are those who bless you, and cursed are those who curse you."*** (NUMBERS 24:9)

Every week, on Shabbat in the synagogue, we pray that God provides our leaders with wisdom and the guidance they need to make the right decisions.

The synagogue in the growing community of Yakir

Pinchas

Numbers 25:10 – 30:1

Every week, on Shabbat in the synagogue, we pray that God provides our leaders with wisdom and the guidance they need to make the right decisions.

"*The Lord said to Moses, Go up into this mountain of Abarim and see the land that I have given to the people of Israel* " (Numbers 27:12). So begins a moving dialogue between God and Moses towards the end of Moses' life. Everything that happens in the remaining chapters of Numbers and all of Deuteronomy actually takes place in the last year of the Israelites' stay in the desert, just prior to their entry into the Land of Israel. And, with this verse, God instructs Moses as to the last days of his own life. Like Aaron, God will guide Moses up a mountain and there he will die. But, prior to his death, Moses will be able to see the entire Land of Israel spread before him, a land that he yearns to enter but God prevents him from doing so.

The actual occurrence of this event is recorded in Deuteronomy chapter 34. Moses ascends Mt. Nebo, on the Abarim, and is able to see, miraculously, the entire Land of Israel.

But what is most interesting in this section of Numbers is not God's instruction to Moses, but Moses' response to God. He does not argue with God nor plea for his life. Instead, his first concern is the continued leadership of the Children of Israel. With this reaction, Moses proves to be the quintessential leader, a man whose very being is intrinsically connected with his concern and sense of responsibility for the nation, above and beyond his own selfish concerns for his life and death.

Moses asks God to appoint a man ***"who shall go out before them and come in before them, who shall lead them out and bring them in, a shepherd for the flock that is the Children of Israel"*** (Numbers 27:16-17). And God instructs Moses to appoint Joshua to this job.

Note that it is not God who appoints Joshua, but Moses who does so, in accordance with God's command. For Moses is, first and foremost a man, and his concern is for a man who will lead the nation. God clearly remains in charge and it is the function of the leader to heed God's will in leading the nation. In fact, Moses' charge to Joshua is: ***"Be strong and courageous...It is the Lord who goes before you, He will be with you, he will not leave you or forsake you."*** But it is Moses who encourages Joshua and who charges him with his mission: ***"You shall go with this people into the land that the Lord has sworn to their fathers to give them, and you shall put them in possession of it"*** (Deuteronomy 31:7-8).

It is amazing how God is often used as a crutch by people who try to evade responsibility. We can sit back and let things run their own course, they will often say, for God is in charge. But Moses did not see things that way, and neither did God. Real, human leadership was needed for the Children of Israel and Joshua was going to have to lead his people into battle. Did that mean that God was not part of the plan? Of course not. But man needed to take responsibility, and the leaders needed to be responsible for the people and for guiding the people in the way that God intended.

Moses wanted to make sure that a worthy leader was appointed to replace him before he died. And that leader, Joshua, was the man who actually brought the Children of Israel into the Land of Israel. Our current leaders are no Moses and Joshua. But every week, on Shabbat in the synagogue, we pray to God to provide our leaders with wisdom and the guidance they need to make the right decisions. That our leaders may have the wisdom and the faith that Joshua had, to do what is right for the Nation of Israel and assist us in settling the Land of Israel, as God has commanded.

*Through his personal experience,
Joshua can help the Children of Israel connect to the land.*

Young people of Naaran work the land in the Jordan Valley

Matot

Numbers 30:2 – 32:42

The people of Israel are the only people in the world who were exiled from their land for 2,000 years and yet remained intact as a people and as a faith.

Numbers chapter 32 describes an interesting encounter between the tribes of Reuben and Gad and Moses. Having just conquered land to the east of the Jordan River, they request permission to settle permanently in this area, in the Gilead and Bashan, an area rich in grazing land and so vital to these two tribes of many cattle. Moses' initial response is a a distressed one.

"Shall your brothers go to the war while you sit here? Why will you discourage the heart of the people of Israel from going over into the land that the Lord has given them?" (Numbers 32:6-7)

Moses then reminds them of the sin of the spies who had returned from the Land of Israel and spoke ill of the land, causing the people to doubt the success of their imminent entry. God's response, of course, was to punish the people and delay the entry for an additional 38 years. Moses fears that if Reuben and Gad remain in the land east of the Jordan, the rest of the people will refuse to enter. After years of experience with the Children of Israel, Moses is quite aware that the littlest provocation can instill fear and lack of faith in the people.

As a result, he continues, ***"For if you turn away from following him, He will again abandon them in the wilderness, and you will destroy all these people"*** (NUMBERS 32:15).

While Moses' fear of angering God seems very legitimate, and his fear that Reuben and Gad's actions might have a negative influence on the people is logical, the last phrase which indicates that the Nation of Israel would be destroyed seems a bit extreme. After all, the nation survived its first delay. Why wouldn't it survive an additional one?

Remember, however, that at this point in time, Moses is close to his death and God has already told him how he will die (NUMBERS 27:13). An entire generation has already died in the desert, those adults who had actually experienced the Exodus from Egypt and the revelation at Sinai. The only people who were adults at these two seminal events who are still alive and who will actually enter the Land of Israel are Joshua and Caleb, those valiant spies who were rewarded because of their faith in God and their love of the Land. If these individuals remain in the desert another generation, no one who enters the land will have experienced the Exodus and Sinai. And it is this vital detail that threatens the continued existence of the nation.

The people of Israel are the only people in the world who were exiled from their land for 2,000 years and yet remained intact as a people and as a faith. What kept us going all those years was the fact that we had the Torah, the Bible, as a guide through the years of exile, and we had a land to yearn for. But those two elements, Bible and Land, had to be linked together, experientially, in some way, in order for the connection to last for eternity.

Joshua's entry into the Land will mark a real departure from the sort of Divine leadership that the Children of Israel have experienced in the desert. The miraculous parting of the Red Sea, the Manna from Heaven and a host of other miracles will give way to a more natural existence in the Land of Israel. And this is reflected in the very real battles that Joshua will fight in the conquest of the Land. But Joshua is equipped to do this because of the spiritual experiences he has witnessed since leaving Egypt.

Joshua leads the people into the land, having personally experienced the Exodus, the revelation at Sinai, and indeed all the wars and tribulations of the desert. Through his personal experience, he can help the Children of Israel connect to the land, and experience the meaning of freedom from slavery, of receiving the Torah. Through Joshua, the link is preserved and passed on forever.

When one's loved one has died and someone is, in fact, at fault, albeit accidentally, the relative cannot help but blame him and want to avenge his loved one's death.

The cemetery of Karnei Shomron

Masei

Numbers 33:1 – 36:13

The Bible recognizes the most basic of human passions, but limits them in order to force human beings to control their behavior.

Chapter 35 details the rules of cities of refuge that are established throughout the Land of Israel, three on the eastern side of the Jordan and three on the western side. Only one who kills someone by accident is entitled to seek refuge in such a city. If someone has intentionally killed someone, or used a weapon or a dangerous tool to strike someone, he is considered to have killed intentionally and is not eligible for protection.

These six cities of refuge are part of the 48 Levite cities which are set aside within the various tribal territories for the Levites who do not inherit any territory of their own. The Levites' main job is to serve God in the Temple, but they also teach the people throughout the land.

It is interesting, therefore, that these six cities of refuge are home to two very different sorts of people: accidental killers and Levites. In practice, however, the cities of refuge often offer temporary refuge to intentional killers as well:

"Then the congregation shall judge between the manslayer and the avenger of blood, in accordance with these rules. And

the congregation shall rescue the manslayer from the hand of the avenger of blood, and the congregation shall restore him to his city of refuge to which he had fled, and he shall live in it until the death of the high priest who was anointed with the holy oil." (NUMBERS 35:24-25)

When someone has been killed, the killer flees to the city of refuge. However, a trial takes place and the congregation, represented by the courts, will judge according to the rules listed in this chapter, whether the homicide was indeed accidental or not. If they rule it to be accidental, then the killer will be returned to the city of refuge and will, therefore, be protected from the relative who seeks vengeance for the death of his kin. This situation continues until the death of the high priest, at which time the killer is free to leave the city of refuge and the avenger of blood is prohibited from taking revenge.

It is interesting to note that there is full legitimacy for the avenger to take the life of the killer, even if the homicide was accidental. While society judges the killer leniently and his life is spared, the relative is entitled to avenge the death of his relative anywhere outside of the city of refuge.

This arrangement seems odd to the modern ear but is actually quite brilliant. When one's loved one has died and someone is, in fact, at fault, albeit accidentally, the relative cannot help but blame him and want to avenge his loved one's death. The Bible does not criticize this very basic feeling; however, it limits it severely. The avenger is not allowed to enter the city of refuge and he is not allowed to avenge the death of his relative after the death of the high priest. While the Bible recognizes the most basic of human passions, in limiting them it is forcing the human being to control his behavior.

However, should the accidental killer leave the city of refuge, he is no longer protected. What would possess the killer from leaving the city of refuge and risking his life? Only if he were so arrogant as to not take seriously the degree of pain that he has caused to the avenger. Forcing him to remain in a city of refuge, therefore, represents a very clear statement to the killer – ***"you may not have intended to kill someone but as a result of your carelessness, someone lost his life. You must take this seriously. You must understand the pain of the people the victim left behind and you must be exiled from your loved ones yourself. For only in this way can you begin to understand the tragedy that you have wrought upon others."***

The presence of the Levites, therefore, serves a very important function. As teachers of the nation, they are in the best position to assist the accidental killer in understanding the tremendous harm he has caused. The city of refuge, serving as a Levite city as well, is, therefore, the best place for the accidental killer to contemplate his actions and to repent for his carelessness. Upon his departure from the city, he should have achieved a higher spiritual level and be ready to enter society once again.

Moses takes the time to address the people of Israel, reviewing their time in the desert, before they enter the Promised Land.

The desert view from Nofei Prat

Devarim

Deuteronomy 1:1 – 3:22

As God's promise of exile as punishment for sin has taken place, so too, His promise of redemption after a lengthy exile will take place.

This portion begins the final book of the Five Books of Moses, the Book of Deuteronomy. The Children of Israel are in the final weeks before their entrance into the Land of Israel. Moses is approaching the final days of his life. And he takes the time to address the people of Israel, reviewing their time in the desert, teaching them the messages that they must remember and internalize before they enter the Promised Land.

This Shabbat, though, also marks the final Shabbat before the 9th of Av, the saddest day on the Jewish calendar. On this day, the first temple in Jerusalem was destroyed by the Babylonians some 2,500 years ago. On this same day, the second temple was destroyed by the Romans close to 2,000 years ago. Throughout Jewish history, this day has been marked by suffering and anti-Semitism. The expulsion decree issued by King Ferdinand and Queen Isabella of Spain in 1492, which forced all the Jews of Spain to flee or convert to Christianity, took effect on the 9th of Av. Some of the most horrible Crusade massacres of Jewish communities took place on the same day. On this day we fast and pray, we remember our terrible history and ask God to bring the Messiah and rebuild the Temple as quickly as possible.

On the 9th of Av we also read the book of Lamentations, that terribly poignant description of the destruction of the First Temple written by Jeremiah, an eye-witness to the events he describes. The Book of Lamentations begins with the Hebrew word *"Eicha"* meaning *"how?"* We chant the Book of Lamentations out loud in the synagogue, sitting on the floor with the lights dimmed, and the tune used is an ancient, mournful one.

In the first verses of the Book of Deuteronomy, the same word *"Eicha"* appears (DEUTERONOMY 1:12). Moses is relating to the people how he had struggled against the burden of leadership, how their rebelliousness and lack of cooperation caused him to request assistance. And yet, this word *"Eicha"*, is so much more than a simple *"How can I do this?"* It includes a sigh, a feeling of strain, of pain, even.

It always works out that these verses are read the Shabbat before the 9th of Av and our tradition is to read the words of this verse to the same chanting tune of the Book of Lamentations. As if to remind us of the coming fast day.

But, the connection between these verses in Deuteronomy and the Book of Lamentations is far more than the apparently coincidental appearance of the two unique words of *"Eicha"*. I believe the message is far more profound. Throughout the Book of Deuteronomy, Moses tries to inspire the Children of Israel to follow God's word. He tells them that their obedience is essential to their ability to remain in the Land of Israel, to avoid the punishment of exile. From the beginning of the book, Moses emphasizes how hard it has been to keep the people on the right path – his expression of *"Eicha"* tells us that.

In essence, Moses knows from his personal acquaintance with the people, that they will sin, that they will end up in exile. With this one word, *"Eicha,"* he already reflects his understanding that the Book of Lamentations will be written. But the message to us, coming as it does after the destructions have already happened, can be an encouraging one. For even as God's promise of exile as punishment for sin has taken place, so too, His promise of redemption after a lengthy exile will take place. In that pain of the word ***"Eicha"*** lies the promise of a better time. May we live to see those days come to pass.

"Remember the Sabbath day."

Author Sondra Oster Baras teaches Australian Christians about the Jewish Sabbath at a weekday simulated Shabbat meal.

Vaetchanan

Deuteronomy 3:23 – 7:11

For the reading of the Ten Commandments, the entire synagogue rises from their seats to relive that incredible experience at Mt. Sinai so many centuries ago.

Tisha B'Av (the 9th of Av Fast Day) is over and we look ahead. There is a spirit of optimism in the air, regardless of anything else that may be happening in the news or elsewhere. After the weekly Torah portion, we read Chapter 40 of Isaiah, which begins with the words *"Comfort, comfort my people."* And we, indeed, feel comforted.

The Torah portion is uplifting as well. For in this week's portion, we read the Ten Commandments, as repeated by Moses in Deuteronomy. For this section of the Torah reading the entire congregation stands, as if to relive that incredible experience at Mt. Sinai so many centuries ago.

Much has been said about the differences between the wording in both versions of the Ten Commandments – this one and the one that is recorded in Exodus 20. I would like to focus on one difference and an ancient traditional interpretation that guides so much of what we do to this day.

The commandment regarding the Sabbath, Shabbat, begins in Exodus 20:8 with the words: ***"Remember the Sabbath day"***. In Deuteronomy, the verse reads: ***"Observe the Sabbath day"***.

The Midrash states that both of these first words, ***"Observe"*** and ***"Remember"***, were actually uttered by God simultaneously, but the human ear is incapable of hearing this. Therefore, as Moses repeats the commandments, he says each word separately, once in Exodus and once in Deuteronomy.

Our sages carried this idea further and explained the inherent difference between these two words. Remember is a positive word and in fact refers to all those acts that we do on the Sabbath day to remind us of the meaning of the day. Foremost among these is the Kiddush ceremony. Friday night and Saturday noon, we say a special blessing on a cup of wine before beginning the festive meal. The actual blessing is preceded by reciting Scripture. In the evening, we recite Genesis 2:1-3. The following day, we recite the verses regarding the Sabbath from the Ten Commandments in Exodus. Through the Kiddush we sanctify the day and remind ourselves of its significance.

Another set of customs that are derived from this special commandment to remember is the idea of ***"oneg Shabbat"***, literally, the pleasure of Shabbat. Oneg Shabbat encompasses the family meals that we share together, complete with singing, laughter and the telling of stories. As a teen-ager growing up in the US, I well remember the Friday evening gatherings through our youth group that we referred to as an Oneg Shabbat. We met in someone's home and spent hours singing songs from Scripture, listening to a teaching from the weekly Torah portion, and enjoying the cakes and munchies that our hosts put out for us. It was truly a pleasurable way to celebrate the Shabbat!

The word ***"observe"*** and particularly the Hebrew ***"Shamor"*** implies a negative – preserve the day, watch it, so that it not be desecrated. It is this word that reminds us of the commandments to refrain from work (DEUTERONOMY 5:14), to refrain from cooking (EXODUS 35:3) and so many other commandments.

But the fact that these words were said together, that both messages were communicated by God to His people in the Ten Commandments indicates that both are essential to the observance of the Shabbat. On the one hand, we refrain from doing so many of our normal everyday activities. If this were all that Shabbat was about, it would end up begin a day of restrictions, of ***"don'ts"*** and ***"better not's"***. But it is also a day of remembrance of God as the creator, and of the special day He has given to us to celebrate. By the same token, just remembering is not enough either. Without setting ourselves apart from our business concerns, we cannot possibly create the atmosphere necessary for the remembrance.

For the Lord your God is bringing you into a good land...
a land of wheat and barley, of vines and fig trees and pomegranates,
a land of olive trees and honey.

Grove of Date Palms planted near the new homes of Gush Katif refugees in Maskiot

Ekev

Deuteronomy 7:12 – 11:25

As the Bible makes clear, man often fails in life's challenges, but in giving us the Scriptures, God has provided us with the tools we need in every circumstance.

This week's portion is part of Moses' second long speech to the nation, referred to as the speech of the commandments. It includes a great deal of instruction, both with regard to specific commandments and with regard to the overall obligation to follow God's word and obey His commandments. The first verses of Chapter 8 are particularly interesting, however, as they refer to the experience of the Children of Israel in the desert and contrast that experience with what they will be experiencing once they enter the Land of Israel. This entire section, however, tells a very different story about the desert experience than what we have heard until now.

"And you shall remember the whole way that the Lord your God has led you these forty years in the wilderness, that he might humble you, testing you to know what was in your heart, whether you would keep his commandments or not. And he humbled you and let you hunger and fed you with manna, which you did not know, nor did your fathers know, that he might make you know that man does not live by bread alone, but man lives by every word that comes from the mouth of the Lord." (Deuteronomy 8:2-3)

For the first time, we learn that the Children of Israel have actually suffered in the Wilderness, or more accurately, Moses gives credence to their prior complaints for the first time.

When the Children of Israel complained about the Manna and the lack of food, the response was critical indeed: ***"Moses heard the people weeping throughout their clans, everyone at the door of his tent. And the anger of the Lord blazed hotly, and Moses was displeased"*** (NUMBERS 11:10).

The assumption is that the Children of Israel are being petty, complaining about their lack of food variety when they should be grateful that they are eating well and not going hungry. And yet, in this section of Deuteronomy, Moses admits that they were hungry and that Manna was not able to satisfy them.

Another interesting element in this section is Moses' assertion that the purpose of their sojourn in the desert was as a test, to determine whether they were sufficiently committed to God and His commandments. There is no mention of the fact that the Children of Israel were punished for their sins, having listened to the slanderous words of the spies against the Land of Israel.

The context of this speech, however, is quite different from the previous descriptions of similar events in the Book of Numbers. The Children of Israel are just weeks away from entering the Land of Israel. Moses is addressing the nation and his perspective is forward-looking. Although he does refer to events of the past, his purpose is to prepare the nation for the challenges they will face when they enter the Land.

And the most significant challenge of all is the potential influence of the Canaanite nations residing there and, in particular, their pagan beliefs. It is, therefore, critical that Moses stress those aspects of the past forty years that will best equip them for their newest challenge. Throughout their desert experience, the

Children of Israel felt the pull to return to Egypt, and Moses needed to enable them to understand the advantages of freedom, which is accompanied by servitude to God. Therefore, it was critical that the Children of Israel be reliant upon God for their food and water and understand that simple food and water from God as free persons is preferable to watermelon and fish in Egypt as slaves.

Now, as they approach the Land of Canaan, their suffering is acknowledged because the benefits of the Land of Israel derive from its fertility and the wealth of its produce.

"For the Lord your God is bringing you into a good land, a land of brooks of water, of fountains and springs, flowing out in the valleys and hills, a land of wheat and barley, of vines and fig trees and pomegranates, a land of olive trees and honey, a land in which you will eat bread without scarcity, in which you will lack nothing." (DEUTERONOMY 8:7-9)

It is critical for the Children of Israel to understand the advantages of the Land of Israel over the desert as they enter that land and become ready for its unique challenges. However, the richness of the land presents its own challenges:

"Take care lest you forget the Lord your God by not keeping his commandments and his rules and his statutes, which I command you today... Beware lest you say in your heart, My power and the might of my hand have gotten me this wealth." (DEUTERONOMY 8:11,17)

On the eve of their entrance into the Land of Israel, the Children of Israel must adjust their faith commitment to accommodate wealth and the temptations of idolatry, to strengthen their commitment to God, despite the change in their circumstances. As the Bible makes clear, they often fail at this challenge. But in giving us all of these Scriptures, God has provided us with the tools we need in every circumstance.

*Everything must be weighed against
the immutable word of God as expressed in His holy word.*

The Study Hall of the Bat Ayin Yeshiva

Re'eh

Deuteronomy 11:26 – 16:17

Particularly today, it is imperative that we weigh everything we see, every impression we absorb, against the immutable word of God.

This week's portion includes a number of laws pertaining to people who exert an undue influence over others in order to sway them away from obeying God's commandments. The first refers to a false prophet, the second to an individual who sways his relatives or close friends, and the third, to wicked individuals who influence an entire city. In all three cases, the objective of the influencer is to draw people away from God and towards pagan worship. In all three cases, the influencer is punished by death.

The first case is that of the false prophet. In this case, the source of the undue influence is the fact that the so-called prophet is able to perform wonders and uses these so-called miracles to sway others to believe the truth of his words. But God is very clear on this point – if his message is inherently false, then, regardless of the wonders and miracles he may perform, this man will be deemed a false prophet. God has already given us His law, His commandments, and will never change them. If someone should come along and try to change anything fundamental, such as the belief in one God, Scripture tells us clearly that he is not to be believed, regardless of the wonders and miracles he is able to perform.

"But that prophet or that dreamer of dreams shall be put to death, because he has taught rebellion against the Lord your God, who brought you out of the land of Egypt and redeemed you out of the house of slavery...".(DEUTERONOMY 13:6*) [DEUTERONOMY 13:5]

It is God's redemption of the Nation of Israel from Egypt, the parting of the Red Sea and the accompanying miracles, which provide the evidence of God's sovereignty on this earth. Our sages noted that a simple maid present at the parting of the Red Sea experienced a greater revelation from God than the prophet Ezekiel; such was the power and force of that great event. So, no matter the signs and wonders that an individual may be able to perform afterwards, he cannot rescind the messages that God has given us in His Torah.

The second evil influencer is someone who takes advantage of his personal relationships to try and sway someone away from true belief. In this case, it is social pressure which is so dangerous. The friend will begin his evil work in secret (DEUTERONOMY 13:7*) [DEUTERONOMY 13:6] but his influence has such potential danger that he must be stopped before he reaches the masses.

In the third instance, an entire city has been swayed and is worshipping pagan gods. But the process begins with a small few – with wicked persons who are themselves residents of the town (DEUTERONOMY 13:13) and who succeed in influencing the rest of the population. Perhaps, this is a case of a private influencer succeeding with one, and in so doing, spreading his influence further until an entire city is gone.

All three instances present the source and ultimate danger of the negative influence itself. In the first instance, the source of the danger is the natural tendency of human beings to trust miracle-

---

* Deuteronomy 13:5-6 is Deuteronomy 13:6-7 in the Jewish Bible.

workers and their willingness to discard solid faith in the face of the supernatural. The second two instances reflect the power and influence that come from relationships.

It is these sources of influence that speak to us so powerfully in every generation. Particularly today, when so many are attracted to ***"spiritual"*** ways, and miracles both real and imagined are being manipulated by a charismatic few in order to sway entire communities, it is imperative that we weigh everything we see, every impression we absorb, against the immutable word of God. And when modern living is so often characterized by alienation, the influence of one who seems to care, who whispers in your ear until he has swayed you and then has swayed you to sway others, is particularly dangerous. Again, everything must be weighed against the immutable word of God as expressed in His holy word.

Our political leaders would do well to follow the guidelines for the kings of Israel, to ensure their righteousness and the absence of corruption in their kingdom.

The government orders the Expulsion from Gush Katif, banishing thousands from their homes
(Photo: Devorah Horowitz)

Shoftim

Deuteronomy 16:18 – 21:9

Our political leaders would do well to follow the guidelines for the kings of Israel, to ensure their righteousness and the absence of corruption in their kingdom.

In this week's Torah portion, we read about the restrictions placed on a king of Israel.

"Only he must not acquire many horses for himself or cause the people to return to Egypt in order to acquire many horses, since the Lord has said to you, 'You shall never return that way again.' And he shall not acquire many wives for himself, lest his heart turn away, nor shall he acquire for himself excessive silver and gold. And when he sits on the throne of his kingdom, he shall write for himself in a book a copy of this Torah... that his heart may not be lifted up above his brothers, and that he may not turn aside from the commandment..."* (Deuteronomy 17:16-20)

These verses set forth guidelines to be followed by the kings of Israel, to ensure their righteousness and the absence of corruption in their kingdoms. Although, we no longer have kings, our political leaders would do well to follow these rules.

---

* The translation uses the word *"law"* but the Hebrew word *"Torah"* is far more expressive of the actual import of this Scripture, for the King is commanded to actually write his own Torah scroll.

- The prohibition against owning many horses is linked with the prohibition against returning to Egypt. Key here is the idea that God redeemed His people from Egypt – a king of Israel must make sure never to take steps that would lead his people to be enslaved once again.
- The prohibition against many wives is more a political rather than a sexual issue. In ancient times, kings took many wives as a way of cementing relationships with neighboring kingdoms, as a sort of peace treaty. However, the danger is that these wives will lead the king astray, that the foreign cultures these women bring with them into the kingdom will influence the king away from God's word and the Jewish way. Today this can easily translate into a word of caution against unhealthy relationships with neighboring nations.
- The prohibition against too much silver and gold is designed to prevent corruption. If a king does not own too much, he cannot be swayed by money and financial power.
- And finally, the king is commanded to write his own copy of the Torah and to keep it at his side, to read it and study it and follow the commandments. A king, or any political leader, must be a God-fearing man and he must avoid arrogance at all costs. If he seeks God's counsel in political decisions, he will ultimately do the right thing.

One of the earliest examples of a king who was not careful of these prohibitions and was corrupted by them is King Solomon. While Solomon was a righteous and God-fearing man, by the end of his reign he had gone astray.

"Now King Solomon loved many foreign women, along with the daughter of Pharaoh: Moabite, Ammonite, Edomite, Sidonian, and Hittite women. from the nations concerning

which the Lord had said to the people of Israel: 'You shall not enter into marriage with them, neither shall they with you, for surely they will turn away your heart after their gods.' Solomon clung to these in love. He had 700 wives, who were princesses, and 300 concubines. And his wives turned away his heart. For when Solomon was old his wives turned away his heart after other gods, and his heart was not wholly true to the Lord his God, as was the heart of David his father" (I KINGS 11:1-4). He took many wives, he built palaces and filled them with silver and gold. His heart was righteous but his many wives and all the trappings that came with them, led him astray.

Today, we are frequently witness to the corruption of leaders, both in Israel and around the world. It pains me when a former prime minister of Israel is on trial for corruption and bribery. Many point to the unhealthy connection between wealthy political donors and political leaders, whose judgement may then be clouded by the undue influence of their wealthy patrons.

One of the most painful experiences of recent years has been the Disengagement — the expulsion of Jews from their homes in Gush Katif. Many have wondered how Ariel Sharon, the political leader of the settlement movement, could turn against his people in such a terrible way. Was he eager to become the darling of the left, in order to avoid possible criminal indictment on bribery charges? Was he seeking consensus admiration to feed a growing ego? We will never know. But we can certainly say, that he was not a leader who kept the Torah at his side, who understood at the deepest level that the Land of Israel was given to the People of Israel by God and that it was for him to serve the nation as a servant of God.

If the leadership of Israel and of the world followed the basic four principles outlined in this portion, the world would be a far better place.

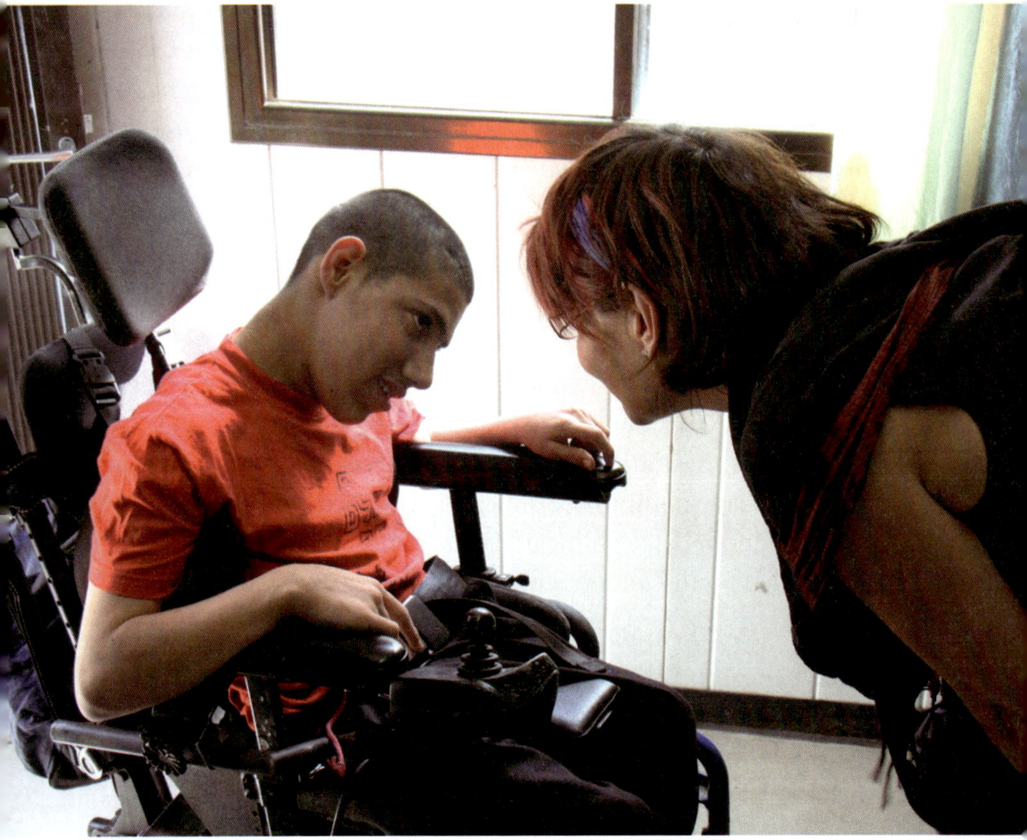

He is a human being with dignity.

A special-needs child with a CFOIC Heartland supporter at Heart of Benjamin in Ofra

Ki Tezeh

Deuteronomy 21:10 – 25:19

The Bible applied to its time and it is in that context that it must be read, but it is also an eternal book, applicable to those of us living thousands of years after it was first written.

This week's Torah portion includes the largest number of commandments of any other weekly portion. Beginning with Chapter 21 verse 10 and proceeding through the end of Chapter 25, verse after verse is filled with situations and the rules of practice that are applicable.

As I read through the verses, one struck me in particular: ***"Do not deliver to his master the servant who is escaped from his master to you. He shall dwell with you, among you, in that place which he shall choose in one of your gates where it is good for him. Do not oppress him"*** (Deuteronomy 23:16-17*) [Deuteronomy 23:15-16].

As I read this I was immediately reminded of the terrible blight of slavery that was so much a part of American society in the 18th and 19th centuries. The abolitionists were very active in opposing slavery and established the Underground Railroad, a system of volunteers who helped smuggle slaves north to freedom.

A common statement of the slave-owners was that slavery was mentioned in the Bible, that it was condoned by God. The

* Deuteronomy 23:15-16 is Deuteronomy 23:16-17 in the Jewish Bible.

Bible does refer to slavery as an existing institution in Biblical times, which it was. But through the verses in this Torah portion, we see the fundamental difference between Biblical slavery and American slavery of the 18th and 19th centuries. The Bible makes it very clear that it is the master's responsibility to make his servant comfortable. He must feel at home and he must be treated well. In reality, a Biblical slave is essentially a servant. He is certainly not a possession.

When slaves escaped their masters in the US, the law required that they be returned to their masters even if they had escaped to parts of the country where slavery was illegal. This was because a slave was considered property and one had an obligation to restore stolen or lost property.

The Bible makes it very clear. A slave is not property. He is a human being with dignity. And if he is not happy and escapes, he may find refuge with someone else. No one can ever force him to go where he does not want to go.

But there remains the more fundamental moral question – how is it that the Bible seems to condone slavery when it seems so morally repugnant to us? I believe that many of the rules and regulations in the Bible relating to social issues take into account existing circumstances and then impose some sort of moral restriction upon them. Nowhere in the Bible does it say that slavery is a good thing. Yet, there are rules and regulations that apply to slavery, so clearly it is a tolerated phenomenon. But the rules do reflect a moral guideline to treat the slave well, to enable him to have a day of rest, etc. Clearly, it would have been impossible to eradicate an institution so deeply imbedded in society at that time, but by restricting it, the moral compass is there. And, over the centuries, man developed enough of a moral compass to recognize that slavery is wrong and abolish it.

Similarly, the verses at the beginning of the portion referring to a soldier taking a woman for himself from among the captives, involve moral guidelines imposed upon a dubious behavior norm. While to our modern sensibilities, this seems like legalized rape, in context, it is a very moral set of scriptures. Rather than allowing a man to follow the norms of the day and literally grab and rape any woman he pleases from among enemy captives, a man must marry the woman, not rape her. And he must treat her well and allow her to mourn her family who fell in the war. He must see her in her mourning attire, not looking her attractive self and then decide he still wants to marry her. He must see something about her character that is attractive, not just her looks.

The Bible is an eternal book, applicable to those of us living thousands of years after it was first written. But it is also a book that applied to its time and it is in that context that it must also be read.

Our relationship with God is inherently connected to our presence in the Land of Israel and the blessings that God will bestow upon us when we settle and farm that land.

A Jordan Valley farmer shares the joy of a new crop with Dutch Christians

Ki Tavo

Deuteronomy 26:1 – 29:8

Our relationship with God is inherently connected to our presence in the Land of Israel and the blessings that God will bestow upon us when we settle and farm that land.

This week's portion opens with the ceremony of first fruits that is performed in the Temple, after the Children of Israel have entered the Land of Israel.

"When you come into the land that the Lord your God is giving you for an inheritance and have taken possession of it and live in it, you shall take some of the first of all the fruit of the ground, which you harvest from your land that the Lord your God is giving you..." (Deuteronomy 26:1-2)

There are a number of words in these first verses that provide the focus for the entire section. The fact that the land has been given to Israel by God is mentioned twice in these two sentences, clearly as a means of emphasis in this chapter. Also, the word translated as inheritance in the first verse, is actually the Hebrew word ***"Nahala"***, which includes the concept of territory. In other words, Nahala is a piece of land designated as the rightful possession of the Jewish people, in essence an inheritance from God.

Following this introduction, the instruction is given to bring the first fruits to the Temple and recite a specific statement which begins with the acknowledgement of Jewish history, the enslavement of the people in Egypt, the Exodus brought about by God, and the entrance into the Land of Israel, made possible by God who has granted the people this ***"land flowing with milk and honey"*** (Deuteronomy 26:9).

This, then, is a thanksgiving ceremony in the fullest sense of the word. It is not only a ceremony which thanks God for the harvest and for the richness of the fruits. It is also, and perhaps primarily, a thanksgiving for the entire process of Jewish history, for the fulfillment of the process that began with the Exodus and culminates with the bringing of the first fruits in the Land of Israel. It emphasizes the fact that the Exodus was not completed with the Revelation at Sinai, which was certainly a monumental event, when the Children of Israel became a people and when they cemented their relationship with God in an everlasting covenant. For it is only when they enter the Land of Israel, take possession of it and farm it, that the process is truly completed, that the nation is truly free to worship God and settle in their own land. (It is worth comparing this process to the antecedents of the Thanksgiving holiday in the US – a holiday that has always symbolized not only a successful harvest but a sense of entitlement to the land that became the USA.)

These verses speak powerfully to me today in many ways. Even as some Jews question the extent to which Judaism is a nationality or a religion, this verse makes it clear that one cannot be divided from the other. For our relationship with God is inherently connected to our relationship with Him as a people, and our worship in the Temple, which functions as the epicenter of the relationship with God, is inherently connected to our presence in the Land of Israel and the blessings that God will bestow upon us when we settle and farm that land.

The connection between the Jewish people and the Land of Israel is not just a spiritual connection — it is a physical one. The presence of the nation in the land is wrapped up with the experience of tilling the land and bringing forth its fruits. The Bible is replete with the rewards that the People of Israel will reap if they remain true to God's word, and those rewards revolve around the blessings of the produce of the land (Deuteronomy 11:13-17).

The people of Israel, the Land of Israel and the faith of Israel are all intertwined.

There is no Jewish religion without Jewish nationalism and there is no Jewish nationalism without the Jewish religion. And when nationalism and religion come together in the Land of Israel, we have a great deal to be thankful for.

The strong desire of these pioneers to rebuild an independent nation in the Land of Israel and the reconnection of so many of them with the Bible was actually a spiritual event.

The children of Shadmot Mechola at their after-school Bible classes

Nitzavim

Deuteronomy 29:9 – 30:20

The first initiative towards repentance must come from man himself, but once a man begins the process, God will assist him in continuing.

This week's portion includes Moses' last speech to the nation before the final poem that is Chapter 32 and the blessings in Chapter 33. Chapter 30 is often referred to as the ***"Return"*** chapter, including, as it does, references to both a physical and spiritual return to God and the Land of Israel. But a close examination of the verses in this chapter reveals a confusing sequence of events.

The first verse of Chapter 30 sets the stage – the blessings and curses have already come to pass. The Nation of Israel has already settled in the Land and enjoyed its blessings, but has also sinned and been exiled, and the land has been decimated, as predicted in Chapter 28. At this point, there will be a return to God, a repentance that is initiated by the people themselves. In the first verse, God promises that ***"you call them to mind among all the nations where the Lord your God has driven you."*** The actual Hebrew phrase for ***"call them to mind"*** is literally, ***"return to your heart."*** Using the same word ***"return"*** that will figure so prominently in this chapter, the stage is set for an introspection, a reminder of the blessings and the curses and the covenant set forth in chapter 28. The second verse is clearer: ***"And return to the Lord your God, you and your children, and obey his voice in all that I command you today, with all your heart and with all your soul."*** The initial awakening will bring in its wake repentance, a return to God.

The following verses speak of a physical return – God will return the people of Israel from their exile among the nations to the Land of Israel. But verse 6 goes back to a more spiritual return: ***"And the Lord your God will circumcise your heart and the heart of your offspring, so that you will love the Lord your God with all your heart and with all your soul, that you may live."*** (DEUTERONOMY 30:6)

This verse, in fact, raises a number of questions: If the entire process begins with a spiritual return, as noted in the first two verses of the chapter, what does this second return signify? And if the initial return is initiated by the people themselves, why does God have to get involved and help the return along with the circumcision of the heart mentioned in verse 6?

A number of classical commentaries interpreted this set of verses as indicating that the first initiative towards repentance must come from man himself, but once a man begins the process, God will assist him in continuing the process. Nachmanides, a 15th century Spanish Jewish commentator, took this idea further. He noted that these verses had not yet come to pass, that they refer to a Messianic age. He believed that the initial spiritual return would bring about the physical return that the Messiah would herald and, at that point, the human inclination towards good and obedience to God's commandments would become natural. The circumcision of the heart refers to a supernatural event that will return man to the state of Adam in the Garden of Eden before the first sin. Nachmanides quoted Jeremiah 31:32* [JEREMIAH 31:33] and Ezekiel 36:26-27, both of which refer to a change of heart that will bring the nation closer to God and to His commandments.

In recent years, commentators have taken a new look at these scriptures in light of the development of modern Zionism and the subsequent establishment of the State of Israel. The physical

---

* Jeremiah 31:33 is Jeremiah 31:32 in the Jewish Bible.

return noted in verses 3-5 has indeed taken place. But what of the spiritual return? Did that precede the physical return? And what of the fact that the main motivation behind the Zionist movement was secular, deriving from a need to solve the horrors of anti-Semitism, to provide a safe haven for the Jewish people. Indeed, most of the early Zionist pioneers were atheists!

Rabbi Abraham Isaac HaKohen Kook was probably the most influential of the early Zionist rabbis. He believed that while the declared motivation of the Zionist pioneers was secular, it actually derived from a deep spiritual core, a seeking of the soul itself for a return to God and to His Land. He believed that the strong desire of these pioneers to rebuild an independent nation in the Land of Israel and the reconnection of so many of them with the Bible was actually a spiritual event, despite their protests to the contrary.

Perhaps therefore, these verses can be seen as referring to the process that is currently happening in Israel. The original return is a return to God, but not necessarily a conscious return, for there is no change of heart. But God picks up on this initiative in order to return us physically to our land. But the final return to God takes place once we are in the Land – only then will there be a circumcision of the heart and a total return to His ways.

Of course, there were always Religious Zionists who felt the stirring to return to the Land as part of a spiritual return to God, Jews who prayed fervently for a return to Zion and Jerusalem. And perhaps it is the presence of these religious Jews in the land, alongside the secular, that is enabling the final spiritual return to take place. And that return is happening, daily, as more and more secular Jews seek out their traditions and their roots, as more Bible study is taking place in Israel than ever before. It is unclear how long the process will take. But we pray daily and fervently for God to bring His promises to total fulfillment, as quickly as possible.

Assemble the people, men, women, and little ones.

Children of Hemdat in the Jordan Valley

Vayelech

Deuteronomy 31:1-31:30

The Bible says that the stranger within our gates should be invited and we wanted to make sure our modern-day, loving "strangers" were included as well.

Deuteronomy 31:11-12 records a very special commandment: ***"You shall read this law before all Israel in their hearing. Assemble the people, men, women, and little ones, and the sojourner within your towns, that they may hear and learn."***

At the end of the seven year cycle, at the close of the Sabbatical year, all of Israel is to gather during the Feast of Tabernacles and hear the Torah read aloud. It was customary for the King of Israel to read selected verses from the Torah. What an impressive gathering it must have been!

The conclusion of the Sabbatical year is selected as the time for this special gathering. The gathering itself combines two key elements — the presence of the nation before the King of Israel and the commitment of the nation to the God of Israel, as symbolized by the reading of the Scriptural verses. It is right and fitting that this be a special event — not an annual event but an event repeated only once in seven years.

The selection of the time for this event at the conclusion of the Sabbatical year is interesting indeed. Farmers will have just completed a time of rest, when the struggles of planting and the hopes and fears for the harvest were put on hold for a year. The nation will have lived for one year on the basis of previous years' harvests, relying on the goodness of God to get through the year. It is quite possible that the farmer will have dedicated more time during that year for Bible study and other spiritual endeavors in place of the usual farming burdens.

Indeed, the sabbatical year is observed in similar ways today, especially by religious farmers. I know of some who literally take the year off and spend the time studying the Bible, as well as the Talmud, Jewish law and Jewish thought. It is indeed a time of spiritual renewal for so many.

As the new year begins, however, the farmer will retreat from his more spiritual experience and return to the earthly one. What an important time, therefore, to repeat the promises of God and His injunctions to remain faithful to His word. As the nation returns to its earthly involvements, it is reminded of the spiritual basis of their work and of their existence.

Many years ago, when I first came to Israel, my family was present at the renewal of this custom. We had small children and we brought them all, so that we could fulfill the complete spirit of this message. Thousands gathered at the Western Wall, the closest we could get to where the Temple once stood, and the President of Israel, then Chaim Herzog, read aloud from the Torah. The Chief Rabbis and other dignitaries were present. It was indeed an awesome experience.

Every seven years since then the ceremony has taken place. I particularly remember one such ceremony, a number of years ago, during the height of the Intifada. At that time, a few of us who were involved with Christian supporters of Israel, decided to hold a parallel event which would welcome Christians to this very special occasion. The Bible says that the stranger within our gates should be invited and we wanted to make sure our loving ***"strangers"*** were included. The event was in English and hundreds were there. Just as the prayers were closing, the Mosque began its call to prayer, blasting out its sounds as if to drown us out. But many had brought shofars and at that very moment, began blowing them with such gusto. It was indeed a memorable event.

Once again, I will close my comments with a prayer for the temple to be rebuilt and become, once again, a focus for prayer for the entire world. ***"For my house shall be called a house of prayer for all peoples."*** (Isaiah 56:7)

Moses understood what so few people understand today -
that we are unable to understand our present if we don't understand our past.

David Goldman exhibits ancient aritfacts in the Kiryat Arba Museum in Hebron

Ha'azinu

Deuteronomy 32:1-32:52

Moses understood what so few people understand today – that we are unable to understand our present if we don't understand our past.

This week we read the Song of Moses, one of Moses' final speeches to the Children of Israel before his death. The only other words Moses speaks to the nation after this are the words of blessing in Deuteronomy Chapter 33. But in Deuteronomy Chapter 32, Moses composes a long poem in which he praises God, discusses His relationship with His people and reviews historical events, some of which are revealed prophetically to him but have not yet occurred.

I would like to focus on two verses, each of which carries messages which speak to me in an especially relevant way.

"Remember the days of old; consider the years of many generations." (Deuteronomy 32:7).

Moses instructs his people to remember their history. In referring to the days of old, he hearkens back as far as Creation – remember the events of the universe from its very beginnings. Understanding the years of a generation implies a deeper comprehension of events, of people, of their actions and the consequences of those actions.

Moses understood what so few people understand today – that we are unable to understand our present if we don't understand our past. If we don't understand the ways of nature and the origins of the universe, and especially the fact that the universe was created by God, we will never be able to comprehend our role as human beings – to serve our Creator. And if we don't evaluate the events of history, the expectations God has from the Jewish people and from all peoples, His judgment over us and the consequences of our actions, then we will be doomed to failure every time.

The second verse that I find meaningful is Deuteronomy 32:15: ***"But Jeshurun (a name for Israel) grew fat and kicked... then he forsook God who made him."***

This verse echoes a set of verses in Moses' earlier speeches to the nation:

"Take care lest you forget the Lord your God by not keeping his commandments and his rules and his statutes, which I command you today. Lest, when you have eaten and are full and have built good houses and live in them. and when your herds and flocks multiply and your silver and gold is multiplied and all that you have is multiplied. Then your heart be lifted up, and you forget the Lord your God, who brought you out of the land of Egypt, out of the house of slavery." (DEUTERONOMY 8:11-14)

As the Children of Israel are about to enter the Land of Israel, Moses warns them of the dangers of prosperity. Even as prosperity is promised as a reward for obeying God's word, it can become a double-edged sword.

When life is good and blessings are abundant – then it is easy for Israel to forsake God, to forget that the source of our blessings is His generosity. When we are in trouble, it is natural to cry out for help. But when things are good, we tend to brag and attribute our success to our efforts alone. We forget that it is God who has blessed us, that it is He who created us, and to Him we owe our gratitude.

If all of Israel, if all of the world, would turn to Him in the height of prosperity, the world would be a better place. The western world is a wealthy world and a secular world indeed.

If all of Israel remembered the lessons of history, even our own recent history with regard to our conflict with the Arabs, and if our entire nation remembered that it is God who has created us and who is responsible for our blessings, we would all hold on to the gift He has given us and never let go. We would all treasure Biblical Israel forever.

Most of us don't even fulfill our own potential. But we can rise to the occasion. We can do the job. We can make the best of what we are and move forward.

After-School Social Services program for teens at risk

Vezot Habracha

Deuteronomy 33:1 – 34:12

As soon as we complete reading the Torah, we begin anew as if to say that the Torah really doesn't end but always begins again, that the cycle continues.

We always read Vezot Habracha on the holiday of Simchat Torah, the day we celebrate the conclusion of the annual cycle of reading the weekly portions of the Five Books of Moses, the Torah. On Simchat Torah we finish the Torah.

The final verses of the Torah are truly moving and have always spoken to me in a very personal way. Moses dies and is buried by God somewhere in the Land of Moab where no one knows his grave site. This was very important, so that no one would turn his grave site into a shrine. Moses was a great man, but a man who was God's messenger. He was not God and it was important that no one would ever worship him as such.

Scripture then attests to Moses' uniqueness as a prophet: ***"And there has not arisen a prophet since in Israel like Moses, whom the Lord knew face to face"*** (Deuteronomy 34:10).

God spoke to Moses directly, not in a dream and not through visions. None of our forefathers, as great as they were, had that same direct and immediate relationship with God. Scripture then mentions ***"the signs and the wonders that the Lord sent him to do in the land of Egypt... that Moses did in the sight of all Israel."*** (DEUTERONOMY 34:11-12).

There is a great sense of loss when Moses dies and Scripture attests to the fact that there never was and will never be anyone like Moses. But the amazing thing is that there is an heir to his leadership mantle. Joshua takes over immediately ***"for Moses placed his hands upon him"*** (DEUTERONOMY 34:9). Joshua is clearly not as great as Moses, and yet he is appointed to the same position – to lead the people of Israel.

None of us is Moses. Most of us don't even fulfill our own potential. But we can rise to the occasion. We can do the job. We can make the best of what we are and move forward. Joshua did this and the people of Israel accepted him as their leader, knowing that he was not on the same level of Moses. They mourned Moses and they moved on.

On the holiday of Simchat Torah, we not only complete the Torah, but we read the first chapter of Genesis. It is as if to say that the Torah really doesn't end but always begins again, that the cycle continues. We prevent the sense of ending that leaving off at the end of Deuteronomy would create. Moses died but the Nation of Israel lived. God's promises to Abraham are repeated again and again as we read through the Torah each year. The people of Israel will never die. Am Yisrael Chai!

Now that Deuteronomy is over,
we start right back
at the beginning of Genesis!

We hope you enjoyed
reading "Shabbat Shalom"
and encourage you
to see all of our other
great Israel resources
at: www.cfoic.com

Afterword

The Jews have always been known as the *"People of the Book"* because of our passion for the sacred Scriptures. Through every trial and tribulation, the Torah has been the heart and soul of the Jewish people and the Nation of Israel has loyally served as the guardians of God's Word throughout the generations. Nearly 2,500 years ago, Ezra the Scribe instituted the practice of reading the Torah publicly in synagogues each Shabbat, which eventually became a set cycle of Torah readings that takes us through the Five Books of Moses each year. Every time the Torah is read, we relive the Revelation at Sinai and we seek to come closer to God who spoke these words directly to our ancestors. Through repetition week after week, year after year, the weekly Portion, or *"Parsha"* in Hebrew, has grounded generations of Jews in the timeless stories, ritual laws and eternal values of the Torah.

In recent years, many non-Jews have turned towards the Land of Israel and the Jewish people in fulfillment of Zechariah's vision for the end of days when the nations of the world will grab on to the garment of a Jew asking to study, saying ***"We will go with you, for we have heard that God is with you."*** Unable to shake 2,000 years of Christian anti-Semitism, many Jews remain skeptical and have rebuffed the advances of Christian Zionists. However, a few courageous individuals have emerged recently with an open mind and a generous heart, seeking an era of reconciliation between the two faiths. At the forefront of these efforts to share the beauty and significance of Israel with the nations is Sondra Oster Baras, Israeli director of Christian Friends of Israeli Communities.

A gifted teacher and passionate leader, Sondra works tirelessly educating Christians about the Jewish communities in the heart of Biblical Israel: Judea and Samaria. For years, Sondra has shared her wealth of knowledge each week about the Torah and the Land of Israel with the supporters of CFOIC Heartland. May the ancient words of Sinai, taught from Sondra's authentically Jewish perspective, penetrate your soul and connect you with generations of loyal followers of the Holy Torah.

Rabbi Tuly Weisz
Director of Israel365 and Publisher
of Breaking Israel News
Ramat Beit Shemesh, Israel

About the Author

Sondra Oster Baras is an Orthodox Jew. She was born and raised in Cleveland, Ohio, and educated at the Hebrew Academy of Cleveland. Upon graduation from high school, Sondra studied Jewish studies at the Jerusalem College for Women in Israel. She completed her B.A. in history and English at Barnard College in New York. She obtained her J.D. at Columbia University's School of Law.

In 1984, after practicing law in New York for a short time, Sondra moved to Israel. Sondra continued her legal career in Israel, after being accepted to the Israeli bar.

In 1985, the Baras' joined Neve Aliza, a group of North American Orthodox Jews that were building a new neighborhood in the small Samarian town of Karnei Shomron. Sondra soon became an active member of the governing board of the group and moved into the new neighborhood in 1987. Shortly thereafter, the first Intifada began, and Ms. Baras was drawn into activities advocating for the settlement movement. Since then, Baras has been an active spokesperson for the communities of Judea and Samaria.

Baras maintained contact with CFOIC Heartland since its inception in 1995, and in 1998, she opened the Israel office in an effort to enhance the organization's activities in support of the communities of Judea, Samaria and Gaza. Since then, Sondra has been the director of the Israel office, coordinating much of CFOIC Heartland's community support programs world-wide.

Sondra Oster Baras currently resides in Karnei Shomron, together with her husband Edward, a computer programmer, and their five children. She can be reached at: sondra@cfoic.com.

About Christian Friends of Israeli Communities

CFOIC Heartland is the only Christian organization to focus exclusively on the communities in the heartland of Biblical Israel. CFOIC Heartland raises funds for the communities and encourages tourism to biblical sites in these areas as well. They have become a resource in Israel for connecting Christians to the people of Biblical Israel, while working in close cooperation with Christian organizations in the Land and with Jewish organizations interested in linking with Christians from around the world. In addition to the main U.S. and Israel offices, there are CFOIC offices in Germany and Holland.

cfoic HEARTLAND
Christian Friends of Israeli Communities

For more information
regarding the work of CFOIC Heartland, please contact:

CFOIC
International Headquarters
P.O. Box 752
Ginot Shomron, Karnei Shomron
Israel
Tel. 972-9-792-0958
Fax: 972-9-788-0108
e-mail: sondra@cfoic.com

CFOIC - USA
North American Headquarters
P.O. Box 50833
Colorado Springs, CO 80949
USA
Tel: 800-647-3344
Fax: 719-683-2041.
e-mail: kim@cfoic.com